Car Accident

A Practical Recovery Manual

For Mary,
The best one
seen at the
worst of times.
Bless you.

Joulie

Car Accident

A Practical Recovery Manual

*for Drivers, Passengers,
and the
People in Their Lives*

JACK SMITH

StressPress
Cleveland, Ohio

StressPress, Cleveland
Copyright © 1995 by Jack Smith
A StressPress Book
Cover & Book Design: Kathleen Katz

Queries regarding rights and permissions should be addressed to:
StressPress Incorporated, 25931 Euclid Avenue, Suite 270, Cleveland, OH 44132
Manufactured in the United States of America

Publisher's Note:
Although the author and publisher have exhaustively researched all sources to ensure the accuracy and completeness of the information contained in this book, we assume no responsibility for errors, inaccuracies, omissions or any inconsistency herein. The ideas, procedures and suggestions contained in this book are not intended as a substitute for consulting with your physician or therapist. Readers should use their own judgment or consult a therapist for specific applications to their individual problems.

First Edition
Publisher's Cataloging in Publication
Smith, Jack, 1943-
        Car accident: a practical recovery manual for drivers,
        passengers and the people in their lives / Jack Smith.
                p. cm.
                Includes bibliliographical references and index.
                ISBN: 1-884189-21-0

        1. Stress (Psychology) 2. Traffic accidents—Psychological aspects. 1. Title

BF575.S75S65 1995
155.9'042   95-68806
                                                                              CIP

95 96 97 98   10 9 8 7 6 5 4 3 2 1

What's in This Book

Welcome

You are probably wondering whether you really need a book like this. Many people have car accidents, and they seem to get over them just fine. Why make a fuss?

I used to think the same thing.

I thought only the "weak" had stress reactions. And it wasn't really a particular event which caused them. The event merely triggered what was bound to surface anyway. And if you paid too much attention to such reactions, it only exaggerated them, prompted a "victim" attitude, or led to other dead ends.

Vietnam brought the first change in my attitude. I saw stress reactions in people whom I knew were not "weak" — people who had worked with me in Vietnam. And the war affected me as well. Vietnam haunted me after I came home. But there was no place to go and no official place to turn. A group of us veterans, guided by Drs. Robert Jay Lifton, Florence Volkman-Pincus and Chaim Shatan, created a model of a place to turn, to heal ourselves. Through that process, my pain and anger became tools. The journey became a way of life.

With Dr. Lifton and Dr. Shatan, I worked to help the American Psychiatric Association recognize what became known as PTSD — post-traumatic stress disorder. Twenty years later, that term is widely known. My early work focused on veterans. Dedicated veterans, who had become professionals, helped set up a network of Vet Centers for Vietnam veterans and nurses. I helped nurture that network.

In 1988, I was invited to Russia with some of those colleagues to begin a process of creating solutions for the problems of soldiers returning from the Afghanistan war. Along the way, individually and in large groups, I worked with survivors of disasters such as flash floods, tornadoes, explosions and airline crashes. I regarded auto accidents as serious but minor.

Then came Adele's accident.

Adele had a bad accident on the Ohio turnpike in which her mother, then 80 years old, was killed. Adele and I worked together as she recuperated. Four months later, she was back driving and working again. And her insurance paid for my time.

As I was working with Adele, several things became apparent to me, which ultimately led to the book in your hands.

First, I realized that all Adele's reactions — though they were initially so intense that her doctor had brought in two psychiatrists to try to calm her — were quite natural.

Second, it was clear to me that Adele had been the agent of her own recovery. I had simply been a coach for her and provided her and her family with some information that I had gained from my years of listening.

Third, I began thinking about why that information and the hard-won wisdom of people like Adele were not easily and widely available to all the others in accidents. I realized that stress reactions, now so obvious after major disasters, tended to be dismissed in their everyday form. Yet the way in which individuals, their families, and the public reacted to more commonplace challenges reflected a miniature version of how they responded to catastrophes.

I reviewed my notes from other accident victims and noted the similarities. I decided to interview the first few of the more than two hundred people I would speak with about their auto accidents. And I realized that each of these people had something to offer. Their understanding could light the way and speed the process of recovery for others.

So I began the book.

As I wrote, memories of a childhood accident that I thought I had gotten over long ago kept intruding. My own "tough it out" attitude had gotten me through, but at a price I became aware of only later.

I had never dealt with Billy's accident. Back in first grade, we used to ride the silver and blue Connecticut Company bus home from school to the projects. Billy always wanted to be the first one out to play. That day, he was riding in the seat just in front of the folding rear doors. He was hanging out the window. As the bus was slowing at our stop, Billy decided to jump out the window. He caught a foot, tumbled, and landed with his legs under the double black wheels. Billy lost his legs, and I willed myself to forget that image. When it came back to me 44 years later, I could see every detail, even the rivets on the side of the bus, the black bolts on the wheels, Billy's face, and his legs disappearing under the still-rolling tires. I realized that while I may have walled off that image, it had never gone away.

Now I knew why, when my 7-year-old stepson would edge close to look over a cliff or lean out a car window, my stomach would suddenly churn and I'd have vertigo; why I would yell at him to get back as soon as I could catch my breath. Yes, it had affected me. That's why it was no accident that I came to write this book.

Along the way, wonderful people educated me in how to turn adversity to good use. So when, on the night this book was finished, a Jeep made a sudden U-turn in front of my car, I knew as I slid into it that, even though it turned out to be just a fender-bender, I was a participant in the processes described in these pages.

This book is an introduction to the natural reactions to a car accident, the early reactions in the first few days and weeks. Since not everyone needs it, I will deal with the strong lingering reactions and what happens down the road in a second volume.

Throughout the book, I have used the words and experience of dozens of people like you who have been through a wide variety of car accidents. Their words breathe life into the book. As you read, you will notice that in a couple of instances, I have referred to the experience of people whose accident or tragedy was not in a car. Although their observations were forged in a different kind of accident, their words so compellingly captured some aspect of the car accident experience that I decided to share them with you as well.

We have all unwittingly collaborated in keeping these natural reactions a secret — burying them and dismissing a piece of ourselves in order to carry on with our lives. I hope the voices in this book illuminate the path for you and your family on your own journey of recovery.

PART ONE:
GETTING STARTED

CHAPTER

1

Megan's Story

"So many times I've sailed around the corner, music blaring and screaming excitedly about something in the future — a date, or a dance or a paycheck. So many times, I can't even count. But, on September 22, 1991, this corner almost caused my death.

"As I flew out the door on my way to work, I heard my father stress, as always, 'Don't speed.' Rolling my eyes at this repeated-a-hundred-times comment, I jumped in my poor brown Toyota Supra and barreled down the driveway. I shifted from first to second to third with ease on my way down the curvy road I'd traveled 1,000 times before. My speed was a steady 35 mph when I passed the rustic white Colonial home on my right. I always slowed down to look at it because of its gorgeous lilac bushes that surround it like a frame. Suddenly, from around the corner, came a gray van on my side of the road. I had nowhere to go but to swerve up onto a bank. I lost control. With no doubt in my mind that I was going to die — I blacked out.

"The next thing I knew, my car was lying on its side and shattered glass was prickling my face. Too stunned to cry, all I could think about was getting out. The car was still running and a Beatles' song was playing. Somehow, I was with it enough to think of my automatic sunroof. With a trembling hand, I pressed the open button. Thoughts ran through my head of the car toppling on me as I tried to get out. However, the idea of the car exploding or another car hitting me told me to get out. I laid

"On September 22, 1991, this corner almost caused my death."

my hands on the pavement and wiggled out the small hole. I noticed the man in the pickup truck behind the van had stopped. He had called the police on his car phone. I sprinted up the hill and wrapped my arms around this stranger's waist. I shook in his arms. From across town, I could hear the police sirens and the roaring of the fire engines.

"The first policeman to arrive was Officer Furello. He looked at my car rocking on its side and then at me, as though he couldn't believe I was alive. With a worried look on his face, he held me, took my petrified face in his hands, and quietly said, 'You're very lucky to be alive.' From his squad car, I called my house. I don't quite remember what I said, but my father arrived instantly. I also called my boyfriend, Aaron.

"At the sight of my father, I began to bawl. I have never seen him so white with fear. Aaron arrived minutes later and he, too, was an abnormal color. People trickled out of their homes to see what the racket was. Firefighters were pouring sand over the leaking gas coming from my car. The man in the pickup truck was speaking to Officer Furello. And all I could do was shake, cry, and attempt, unsuccessfully, to tell what had happened. After the paramedics checked me out, Aaron led me to his car and brought me home, where my friend, Melissa, was pacing the lawn. I began to cry as she embraced me. It was a miracle that I was alive, and I knew it. The only way to show my gratitude at that moment was to cry.

"By the time my parents returned, I had calmed down enough for my father to explain what had happened. The car had been pushed up on the bank, went up a tree 15 feet into the air, nose dived down over a stone wall, catapulted back into the road, and slid on its side for 15 feet.

"Later that evening, after resting all day, I looked up from my dinner plate to find my family staring at me in amazement.

A cold chill ran through me as I realized what they were thinking. My eyes wandered to each one of them. Dad, with tired, worried bags underneath his bright blue eyes, gave me a look of exhausted happiness and returned to his meal. Mom's brown eyes gleamed proudly, as she smiled comfortingly. My little sister, still not quite able to grasp what had happened, didn't know what to do with herself, so she just went back to her dinner. My heart ached at the emptiness of death and the thought of being without family and friends.

"I have a feeling that my perspective on life and death has dramatically changed after this frightening experience."

This book was written for all the Megans and their families in the belief that their stories can help ease the pain and aid the growth of many accident survivors who suffer silently and alone.

2

What This Book Is About: Your Recovery

This book is written for several groups of people affected by serious auto accidents: those who have just been through an accident, their families, and their friends. All these people have their own reactions to the accident and want to help the people they love.

Above all, this book is about taking back your life and your personal power. That means helping you grab the tools within your reach. The "you" may be the survivor of a serious automobile accident, a concerned family member, a friend, or a colleague. The tools are understanding, knowledge, example, and encouragement.

You had an accident, and you took your car to the body shop; now what do you do about the driver?

You can see the damage to your vehicle, but will you pay attention to the hidden impact on your self?

You may not want to talk about it, but if you're now curious to know about your stress reactions after the car accident, this book is for you.

Both sides of that reaction — wanting to get as far as possible away from your reactions, yet being hungry for information to help put them to rest — are what make car accident stress frustrating, complicated . . . and solvable. That's why I wrote the book and why you are reading it — to figure out some of these reactions and move on.

You are the captain of your recovery. No expert has the answers; they lie within your heart.

The impact of an auto accident sends waves of reactions through many people — the people in the accident itself, their families and friends, and the teams of police, firefighters, and EMTs (emergency medical technicians). When it involves a school bus, a carload of children, several cars, or a well-known family, the impact can profoundly touch a whole community. Even when it is a near miss, an accident has an impact on the people involved.

Everybody who has an accident will have some reactions. The reactions may last only a few hours, or even a few minutes in a near miss or a minor fender-bender. But if the accident was more serious, a process will be at work. The "Stress Bill" scale on page 20 enables you to quickly size up the accident you had in terms of its likely consequences.

These car accident stress reactions are normal and expectable. One reason they don't feel normal is that you probably didn't have them before the accident. But they are the normal indicators that your mind, heart, and body are adjusting to the new reality of the accident. If today is very different from the day before the accident, it is because the car accident stress recovery process is at work. Just as your body needs healing, so does your mind.

This book is practical, straightforward, and filled with advice from others who have successfully coped with accidents and emerged stronger people.

Even if I could talk at length with each of you, I could never know exactly what it has been and still is like for you coping with your accident. The pain, the trauma is yours alone, and it's impossible to fully share with anyone else. But in watching the relief that so many people have gotten from unburdening themselves of their pain and reactions to others who have been through a similar trauma, I know that company truly helps. And I know that isolation does nothing to relieve the pain.

As you read *Car Accident: A Practical Recovery Manual*, keep these truths in mind:

- The path you take through these reactions is yours alone.

- Some things may apply to you. Others may not.

- You are the captain of your recovery. No expert has the answers; they lie within your heart.

- If you are open, you will find wisdom in this book that will lend shape to what you have been through and illuminate the path ahead.

- Each step on your journey will change your point of view.

- Some things will make sense now; others may only be apparent later.

- How you pace yourself, and the support you have and are willing to use, will determine your reactions and your outcome.

You are not alone. Your reactions and feelings are quite common, and those feelings form a pattern that flows in stages. In the following pages, earlier survivors have agreed to share — through their words, their pain, their courage, and their experiences — how they have dealt with the feelings you now have. And they want to show you some of what you may encounter on your journey.

If today is very different from the day before the accident, it is because the car accident stress process is at work.

SUMMARY

Everyone has reactions. Your choice is not whether you will have reactions but how you will handle them. This recovery is yours, and the option of how to handle it is yours. But you can rely on those who have made this journey before you to help you through.

CHAPTER

3

This Is a Bunch of Baloney!

By now, some of you are already sighing and shaking your heads.

"I don't have any of those things going on! It's just a car accident. Let's not blow this out of proportion!"

You may be right. Total up your "Stress Bill" on page 20 and if the score is low, then I agree.

However, if your score is in the middle or is high, then you ignore car accident stress at your peril.

Stress studies show that the ability to let stress and feelings *flow* suggests healthy emotional arteries. *Ignored stress* builds up like plaque deposits on your emotional arteries, cutting down oxygen to your feelings. Then, the risk you run is the emotional equivalent of a heart attack. As a cancer patient eloquently put it, "The tears the eyes don't cry are wept by the heart."

One myth about these stress reactions is that if you ignore them, they won't affect you. Often people don't realize there is a cost for failing to recognize, understand, and hasten the healing of these reactions. The myth many people believe is, "If you ignore the stress, it will disappear." Believing that myth supports a related misguided principle — providing preventive help for stress adds "unneeded" costs, mucks around in things "better left alone," and is liable to "stir up things" and just make them worse.

This book is based on an opposite premise — that knowledge, understanding, and support all help people recover faster.

> **One myth about car accident stress is that if you ignore it, it won't affect you.**

While there is truth in the notion that time heals many wounds, how well they heal is another question. Who wouldn't want to properly set a broken leg? Time may heal it, but why risk a limp, gangrene, or permanent disability? This book will help you "set" your recovery from the stress of the accident, and avoid a traumatic stress disorder — the equivalent of a psychic limp.

SUMMARY

Many people believe the myth that if you don't pay attention to car accident stress it won't affect you. In fact, what you ignore can hurt you.

Ignored stress builds up like plaque deposits on your emotional arteries, cutting down oxygen to your feelings.

CHAPTER

4

How to Use This Book

This book is designed for you to use as you need it. Most people will read it in stages. Few people will find that they want to read it straight through. Not all the sections will apply to you.

When you are intensely involved in your reactions to the accident, it is difficult to concentrate for long and easier to focus on just what you need right now. *Car Accident: A Practical Recovery Manual* is designed to help you find and use only that information you need and can handle today.

One quick way to get what you need is to turn to the chapter that seems to fit right now. Then just read the chapter title, the key phrases in large type, and the chapter summary at the end. If you want more information, you can go to a section and read more in detail. Or you can skim the whole book by just reading the key phrases.

The topic headings are clearly identified in "What's in This Book" at the front and in the index at the back. Read the topics and chapters that seem to fit right now. You can read other topics when you are ready for them.

You may find you will read some sections several times or more, finding new insights that you hadn't noticed before. You are in charge of using this book in the way that works best for you.

It is your recovery. Take what you need, when you need it, and leave the rest.

Many of you who have recently had an accident are looking

You are in charge of how you use this book. Use it the way that works best for you.

One quick way to get what you need is to turn to the chapter that seems to fit right now. Read the chapter title, the key phrases, and the summary at the end.

for help in understanding what you have been through and for information that may help make the ups and downs of the roller coaster of responses less steep and less lonely. Chapter Nineteen, "Things You Can Do Right Now," identifies practical steps you can take immediately. The chapters on the phases of reactions will help you better understand the changes the accident has so quickly brought out in you. That will take away some of the fear and concern.

If Your Accident Was Some Time Ago

The book is also useful if you went through an accident some time ago. You may be surprised to find that even after all this time, you still have reactions to that accident. Or you may want to better understand what you have been through, discovering not only what reactions may remain . . . but how well you have done.

If it has been a while since your accident, it will help to read the early sections on Emergency Reactions and take comfort from the fact that some reactions mentioned were yours, while others you didn't have to endure. You may say, "Whew! Thank God I didn't have to deal with that!" The chapters "Lingering Reactions" and "Down the Road" in the second volume of this set will help you better understand where you are now and why.

You may have had your accident years ago, but will be curious, as you look back, to see how well you managed. You can see in retrospect the pattern that your reactions traced through this process. You may find that there are unresolved pieces that remain with you. If so, the book will help you finish your recovery and understand how the accident may still touch your life today. You will see how your life now may even be enriched by the accident and the challenges you have overcome in your recovery.

The book is designed to help you find and use only that information you need and can handle today.

FOR THE CONCERNED OTHER

This book has special sections in several chapters for spouses, family, friends, and colleagues — in short, all the other "concerned" people who are also affected by the accident. These sections detail many of your own reactions to the accident and offer hints for resolving those reactions, *as well as* suggestions on supporting the recovery of those survivors you care about. You will find it most helpful to read the sections addressed to the survivor and follow up with the accompanying section for the concerned other. To be of help to your survivor(s), you must pay attention to your own reactions. Only then can you be a real ally to your loved one(s).

SUMMARY

The book was designed to be read in small doses. Each section can be read without the others. Use it as you need it.

CHAPTER

5

Your Car Accident "Stress Bill"

"There were six of us in the car. But if you listened to the story from each of us, you would think we had been in six different accidents."

How powerful an impact a particular accident will have on you depends on several factors. Some of them you can easily guess, others are not so apparent. And it is not just the accident itself that will influence the reactions. The intensity of your reactions will depend on what happened in the accident; what the consequences are for you; and what you brought in the way of problems, worries, and coping skills to the accident. Rating these factors will give you an idea of your "Stress Bill," the potential impact of this accident on you.

For years, when someone came to me after an accident, I would listen, ask several key questions, and then quickly size up for myself the likely Stress Bill from the accident. By sharing that vision with my client, we could start to grapple together with the problems. The measure I had in my head took into account the research and a good deal of insight from years of listening. The problem was that it was in my head. So I have written this Stress Bill scale down and tested it with many different car accident survivors. It will help you get a quick fix on how serious the situation is for you and the resources you have on hand to cope with it.

Even if your accident was a while ago, find out your Stress Bill. You may be surprised by what you learn from it.

Before you jump to any conclusions about whether you or anyone else is either "overreacting" or "denying," you first need to gauge the size of the "Stress Bill" from the accident.

FOR THE CONCERNED OTHER

If you are close to someone in an accident, add up the Stress Bill first for yourself. It is important that you realize how much this accident has affected you too. When you take the Stress Bill scale, answer from your point of view starting with the time you actually found out about the accident.

If the survivor has completed the Stress Bill scale, ask if they mind sharing the results with you. If they do, go through the Stress Bill scale again, putting yourself in the survivor's place, answering the questions with your knowledge of the accident. Then you won't be in the dark. You will have a fix on your own Stress Bill and the Bill the one you care about faces.

Calculating Your "Stress Bill"

Read each question in order. Think about your accident from the different point of view expressed in each question. Don't worry if your answers seem inconsistent. The Stress Bill scale is designed to look at the experience in different ways. Each question has options which range from 0-3, 0-5, or 0-7. The largest number is the maximum and the minimum is 0. Let your first instinctive response tell you how you rate that aspect of the accident. Give the rating which best reflects how you see that side of the accident.

When you have finished your Stress Bill scale and your "Resource Account" scale, total your ratings for each scale and mark them down.

Your Car Accident Stress Bill

Name:_____

Date of Stress Bill rating:_____

Date of the accident: _____

Time since the accident:_____

Briefly summarize the accident:_____

_____

_____

_____

_____

_____

_____

_____

_____   ☑ Check your
answer

How are you filling out the Stress Bill scale?

As a survivor   ☐

As a concerned other   ☐

As a concerned other in the place of a survivor   ☐

Car Accident Stress Bill Scale

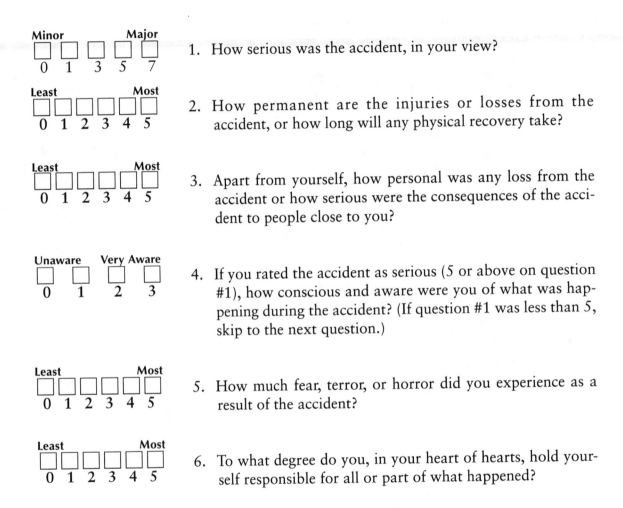

Minor   Major
☐ ☐ ☐ ☐ ☐
0 1 3 5 7

1. How serious was the accident, in your view?

Least   Most
☐ ☐ ☐ ☐ ☐ ☐
0 1 2 3 4 5

2. How permanent are the injuries or losses from the accident, or how long will any physical recovery take?

Least   Most
☐ ☐ ☐ ☐ ☐ ☐
0 1 2 3 4 5

3. Apart from yourself, how personal was any loss from the accident or how serious were the consequences of the accident to people close to you?

Unaware   Very Aware
☐ ☐ ☐ ☐
0 1 2 3

4. If you rated the accident as serious (5 or above on question #1), how conscious and aware were you of what was happening during the accident? (If question #1 was less than 5, skip to the next question.)

Least   Most
☐ ☐ ☐ ☐ ☐ ☐
0 1 2 3 4 5

5. How much fear, terror, or horror did you experience as a result of the accident?

Least   Most
☐ ☐ ☐ ☐ ☐ ☐
0 1 2 3 4 5

6. To what degree do you, in your heart of hearts, hold yourself responsible for all or part of what happened?

7. To what degree do you feel that the negligence, carelessness, or even deliberate recklessness of someone else caused or contributed to the seriousness of the accident?

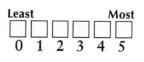

8. What is the impact on you of the challenges posed by the accident? At the high end would be thoughts like, "It seems as if everything I've ever known or believed in somehow got turned on its head because of the accident." At the low end are thoughts like, "The accident had no real effect on me."

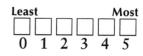

9. How serious were any other previous accidents in your life or other losses in recent years?

10. Rate the other stresses in your life.

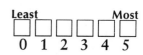

Now add the answers to each of the questions and enter the total here.

Stress Bill Total: _____

Some Reactions You Might Expect

If your Stress Bill total is:

0 - 4   If you had to have an accident, you had the best kind. You won't have significant reactions.

5 - 9   You had a minor accident. You have some reactions but you should be on your way quickly. Be sure to read Chapter Sixteen, "The Near Miss and the Fender Bender." It may also be helpful to read about the signs of stress reactions so you'll know what signs to pay attention to in the reactions you do have.

10-14   You had a real scare and, although you realize how lucky you are, you have a number of reactions. This book will help you sort through where you are now and start you on the way to putting the experience in perspective.

15-19   This accident has had more of an impact on you than you think. You won't just be "over it" in a few days or in a couple of weeks. This guide will be very helpful in putting the pieces together for you and for those close to you. Make the process of recovery an opportunity, not a liability.

20-24   This accident was serious for you. Don't underplay its impact but plan how you are going to maximize your recovery. Use this book again and again. Share it with those close to you.

25 +   Either you have had a severe accident with many reverberations or there are several major things you are trying to cope with besides the accident. Much of your energy will go into coping. You will find yourself with less time or energy for the other things you ordinarily might be doing. You will need plenty of support, so plan on how to get it. Use this book as a guide. You will also want to monitor whether the additional support of a professional can help you get through the rougher parts of this recovery successfully.

Your Stress Bill and the Resources to Cope

How much stress you will feel from your accident is not just some abstract number. It is combination of the stress demands you face from the accident and from the other pressures in your life . . . balanced against the resources you have available to deal with those stresses.

Charles Dickens said it well in an example of how small differences in the balance of income and expenses can have a dramatic effect on outlook. To paraphrase Charles Dickens from his book *David Copperfield*:[1]

Annual Income	$20.00	
Annual Expenses	$19.96	
Result	.04	= Happiness
Annual Income	$20.00	
Annual Expenses	$20.06	
Result	- .06	= Misery

A small difference can dramatically affect the outlook. As the Dickens example illustrates, it's not just the size of the bill that counts; it is the funds you have to pay the bill. So let's get some notion of what is in your "Resource Account."

Your Resource Account

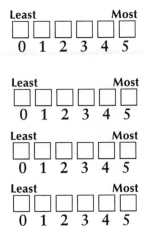

Least   Most
0 1 2 3 4 5

Least   Most
0 1 2 3 4 5

Least   Most
0 1 2 3 4 5

Least   Most
0 1 2 3 4 5

1. How usual is it for you to "carry on" in a crisis, and do you later usually tend to distract yourself — to try and get away — from difficult or painful things?

2. Is it usual for you to reflect on things and figure them out in your mind in a crisis and afterward?

3. How regularly do you let yourself lean on others as supports?

4. How determined are you to deal with things and recover thoroughly?

Now add the answers to each of the questions and enter the total here.

_____ Total   **Your Resource Account Total**

Now look at your totals for the Stress Bill scale and the Resource Account scale. Think of the Stress Bill rating as the bill you got from the accident. Think of your Resource Account as the money you have in the bank to draw against.

You may have noticed that the Stress Bill could total 50 but the Resource Account can only total 20. No matter how much you have in your resource bank, it cannot cover the Stress Bill for a big accident. You are either going to be overdrawn, or you will have to pay the bill over time. That's why both the "carrying on / distraction" and the "reflection" skills are so important. You need both to delay the bill and to make payments on the balance. (For a longer discussion of reflection and distraction, see Chapters Eight, Nine, and Ten.)

Interpreting Your Ratings

Now compare your Stress Bill scale and your Resource Account scale. The Stress Bill represents the demand on your resources right after the accident. How long has it been since the accident? If the accident happened recently, the Stress Bill reflects what you are facing now and will face in the coming months. If your accident occurred over six months ago, your Stress Bill is probably 10-15 percent lower than the Stress Bill scale shows because you have already done some of the recovery work and paid down the bill. Remember, the Stress Bill scale shows the bill you had right after the accident. If your accident was a year ago or longer, your actual Stress Bill now is lower. But we both know that if the initial bill was high, there is some balance due.

I call this your Stress Bill because in some ways it is very similar to the dollar estimate of physical damages to your car (and to you) in the accident. The insurance company estimates the damages done. Even if you never made the repairs, the cost for repair remains, despite the fact that you put it off.

If your original Stress Bill is low, and you have a good balance in your resource account, you can, in effect, write a check right away and be done. The accident should not have long-term effects. But you may want to check out Chapter Sixteen — "The Near Miss and the Fender Bender."

If your Stress Bill scale and the Resource Account scale totals are about the same, then you probably don't want to pay all of the bill at once because you would wipe out your resource account. It might be easier on you to spread the payments out. This book can help you do just that.

If the Stress Bill scale total is greater, and your accident was recent, you are probably feeling pressured, strung out, or, at times, even panicked. Perhaps you are asking, "How am I going to pay this bill?" What follows will help you grapple with the problem and work out a timely payment plan.

> **If your original Stress Bill is low, and you have a good balance in your resource account, you can, in effect, write a check right away and be done.**

If your Stress Bill scale total is double your Resource Account scale total, you share the feelings of someone facing bankruptcy. But all is not lost. The information here will help you avoid emotional bankruptcy.

If Your Accident Was Some Time Ago

You have paid off a good deal, if not all, of your Stress Bill. However, if your original bill was high, you probably still experience effects from time to time. You may want to read the second volume in this series, especially the chapters on the later effects, "Lingering Stress Reactions" and "Down the Road." They can help put in perspective how the accident may affect you even now.

Note that you can have a high Stress Bill without having experienced a devastating accident. That explains why previous accidents, as well as other losses and stresses in your life, are so significant. They draw down your balance so that you have fewer resources available to pay the current bill.

Some people ignore their Stress Bill or put it off. The price paid is that it does not go away. Instead it gathers psychic "interest." Later, when something else happens, the current bill gets laid on top of the long overdue and compounded bill. Then you have that much more to pay off.

Your Individual Stress Bill Questions

Review your answers to the individual Stress Bill questions. Pay close attention to the questions that received the higher ratings. High ratings on the questions about the seriousness of the accident and the closeness and permanence of consequences indicate that you have had a bad accident which ripples with impact throughout your life. High ratings on challenges or personal responsibility questions signal issues that either mean you are going to spend a good deal of time reassembling the pieces, or you will find yourself choking off some aspects of your life in order to manage.

High ratings on negligence mean you are vulnerable to someone else's irresponsibility or recklessness. To recover, you have to face that vulnerability. The trap lies in shifting too much of your attention outward, so you divert resources from the things you can do for yourself and your family, and are left feeling victimized and helpless.

Review your Resource Account ratings. Look particularly at your ratings for carrying on and reflection. It takes both to successfully negotiate the recovery process. What is your pattern? Did you give yourself a high rating on reflection? If not, you probably shy away from reflection. That helps you postpone paying the piper. Even if you do have a pattern of reflection, you need to be able to get away and forget it for a bit. Look at the tips in Chapter Nineteen, "Things You Can Do Right Now."

If your response to one of the first two Resource Account questions is lower than the other, take note. That skill — either distraction or reflection — is the one that is less natural for you. You will want some help in strengthening that ability. If your rating was low on "carrying on" and "distraction," see the section "What to Do — About Sleep Disruptions and Nightmares" in Chapter Nine. If your rating was low on reflection, read Chapters Nine and Ten on reflection and distraction, since your tendency will be to pass over the painful "figuring out" that you need to do to digest the accident.

Your Time Investment

It is going to take some time for you to work through the recovery process after the accident. One of the keys is to know how much of your time this process will take. To get a rough estimate, look at your Stress Bill scale total. Now double that number and add a percentage sign. That percentage roughly reflects how much of your time, right after the accident, will be spent coping with the accident and your other stresses. For ex-

> **The Stress Bill does not go away. It sits there compounding interest until you settle it. If you put it off too long, you may even forget it is there, until another loss or trauma calls up all the unpaid bills that are due.**

ample, a Stress Bill scale total of 5 means only 10 percent of your time will be involved, but a Stress Bill scale total of 25 means that, for a while at least, 50 percent of your time will be taken up with sorting out reactions to the accident.

Clive, a young Englishman living in America, went through the windshield and was badly injured in an accident. For more than a week, it was unclear that he would live at all. Finally he did recover, but he had lost all of his teeth.

One thing he had to look forward to was his forthcoming marriage to Ann. But Ann was becoming worried about the engagement and the prospects for the marriage. Out shopping with Clive to select their china pattern, Ann noticed that Clive kept focusing not on the china but on how it reminded him of what kind of porcelain material he should get his new teeth made out of.

Ann grew upset. Clive was not focusing on her and their forthcoming life together in the way he used to. She had gently nursed him through so many months of recovery. Now he was healed and yet he was still different — "self-absorbed" in some disturbing way. Ann felt he was deliberately letting things remind him of the accident he had supposedly gotten over, and focusing on "stupid" things like what kind of teeth to get.

"Isn't Clive overreacting a bit?" she thought. "Is this a troubling side of him emerging?" Ann and her mother agreed that they would watch and see whether to cancel the wedding.

Were Ann and her mother insensitive and self-absorbed? Was Clive overreacting? None of them had any way to know what was "normal" in this case. Clive didn't know about the time he had to invest in his mind's recovery. Ann and her mother didn't know about their own reactions and the impatience which ignorance of stress reactions promotes. The Stress Bill, plus a calculation of the time investment for recovery as well as a reading of Chapter Fourteen, "The Dumb Things People Say," would together reveal to all three of them how typical all of their concerns and reactions actually were . . . and how easily information could soothe their anxieties.

The effects of a serious accident will be evident for a long time. They will not be overwhelming, but they will make a difference in your life, as they did in Clive's.

As time passes and you absorb the accident and adjust, you will have paid down much of the Stress Bill. There are still times when reactions may catch you unaware. You won't have to spend as much time as you did initially, but you may want to pay attention to the chapters "Down the Road" and "Lingering Stress Reactions" in the second volume in this set.

One difficult realization is that you can't change the accident itself. It's a fact. But you do have the opportunity of keeping it from becoming a greater liability. Even if someone else was at fault and caused great harm, you can keep from becoming a further victim of the accident. If Clive and Ann's engagement had been broken off by lack of knowledge about what reactions were normal, both would have paid dearly in the aftermath of the accident. If you let your life be controlled by the accident or by ignorance of car accident stress, you lose doubly. This guide will help you turn the consequences of your experience into assets during your recovery.

FOR THE CONCERNED OTHER

If you have your own ratings and one for the survivor you care about, you now have a good idea of what both of you are facing. If you have a high Stress Bill, remember that you have to pay your own bill and not just try to be of help to someone else. If you rated the Terror, Challenges, or Personal Responsibility ratings highly, then you have issues to work out with your loved one. Don't presume that because you were not there, you were not deeply affected, too. Read the material for yourself. Then turn to Chapters Fourteen and Fifteen, "The Dumb Things People Say" and "What to Say and Do When You Don't Know What to Say or Do." There you will find out how you can help both of you right away.

If you have a low Stress Bill rating but your survivor has one higher than you thought, pay close attention to what others say in these pages and use it as a guide. First read Chapter Fourteen, "The Dumb Things People Say," to avoid falling into the traps that can make him or her wary of your help.

SUMMARY

Every accident has an emotional bill. It is different for each person. The ratings in this section help you assess your bill for this accident and the resources you have to pay it off. You can also calculate the time investment your recovery will take.

---

[1] "Annual income twenty pounds, annual expenditure nineteen nineteen six, result happiness. Annual income twenty pounds, annual expenditure twenty pounds ought and six, result misery." Charles Dickens, *David Copperfield* (1872). London: Harper, p. 12.

PART TWO:
THE THREE PHASES
OF CAR ACCIDENT
STRESS

Phases

Reactions to an accident follow in three phases:

First Reactions, Digestion, Acceptance

The first two phases will be covered in their own sections. The third phase is explained briefly in this book and then covered in depth in the second volume in this set.

Phase One: First Reactions cover those immediate reactions that begin right at the scene. These are emergency reactions for the survivor and are matched by first reactions in the concerned other. They may last from a few minutes to 48 hours or more.

Phase Two: Digestion covers reactions that set in after the immediate crisis is over. It is in this period that the realization of what has happened (or could have happened) begins in earnest. The digestion phase usually begins 4-48 hours after the accident when the impact sets in. In some cases, it may not hit until sometime later in the first couple of weeks. The digestion phase can last from a few hours to many months, depending on how big the Stress Bill is.

Phase Three: Acceptance is the final phase. Acceptance can be achieved quickly in a minor accident or may take more than a year for a severe accident. Again the Stress Bill is a good indicator. Although I shall talk briefly about acceptance late in this book, an in-depth discussion of acceptance and the journey to that stage is the subject of the second volume in this set.

Now let's look at the first two phases in more detail.

PHASE ONE:
FIRST REACTIONS

Emergency Reactions of the Survivor: Outcry, Shock, and Auto Pilot

Outcry

"Oh, my God!!!!" Elizabeth gasped as she glimpsed and then stared unbelievingly into the rear view mirror at the man and child in the car careening, without slowing, down the hill toward her car, which was stopped at the traffic light.

That outcry is the very first reaction. Almost involuntarily, as the car went out of control, as you saw the other car coming, you cried out, to yourself or aloud:

"Noooooooooooooo!"

Immediately your mind is at work.

"A million thoughts went through my head: 'Oh, God, my children, they need their mommy . . . Eric . . . I just bought this new car . . . That car is blue . . . They're gonna hit me and I can't do a damn thing about it . . . I can't die, I have to get back to work.'" [2]

For others, the recognition has an eerie, almost placid calm.

In the back seat, Earl realized the car was going to hurtle off the bridge. "Suddenly all my petty concerns were gone. 'It's over, I'm dead,' I thought, amazed at how calm I felt."

> **"How quickly I had gone from mom and wife dining with the family to frightened little girl crying in the rain."**

You may fight off the recognition:

"This can't be happening!"

As the awful realization hits that something terrible is about to occur, it ignites a rush of adrenaline. That adrenaline rush — the "fight or flight" response — shuts down many bodily functions (like digestion or drowsiness), and helps tune out feelings and reactions (like pain) not necessary for immediate survival. That's why they're called emergency responses.

Shock

"After the collision I was in total disbelief. I just couldn't believe this had happened to me. Me, the careful driver.

"With the buckled hood staring me in the face, I sat there dazed, not realizing yet that I had hit my forehead on the steering wheel and banged my knee something fierce.

"Traffic whizzed by as the rain pelted the roof of my mangled car. Some cars slowed but none stopped. I even saw a few curious drivers look into my car, which was stretched over two lanes. I started to worry about being hit again. Worry gave way to panic as I realized what had happened. I began to feel claustrophobic.

"Leaving the car triggered tears which mixed with the raindrops. How quickly I had gone from mom and wife dining with the family to frightened little girl crying in the rain.

"Seeing the damage to my car, I knew without a doubt I could easily have been killed. Thank God I was wearing my seat belt.

"I shivered in the cold and mumbled out loud, 'Somebody help me . . . Quit staring . . . It wasn't my fault, please help.' " [3]

For some, the realization of impending disaster comes with the recognition that it is now beyond their control to avoid it. The shock then helps them prepare for the inevitable.

The light was red. There were cars to the right and left of her and others passing through the intersection. She could only stare in horror as the car bore down on her. She watched the driver scrape his wheels against the curb as he came down the hill, trying to slow the car down. But there was little she could do as she gripped the wheel waiting for the crash. It was as if it was in slow motion.

"I just couldn't believe this had happened to me. Me, the careful driver!"

Operating on Automatic Pilot

For others, shock triggers automatic responses that help them cope with the immediate danger.

Driving into the morning sun, Tom pulled the visor down to block the blinding light. Tom, a doctor, was thinking about a critical meeting at the conference he had just attended. Focused on his thoughts, he drove in the left lane, hurrying to the mall with his daughter so she could buy a birthday present for a friend. With alarm, he realized that, without signaling, the car in front was stopping to turn left. At 35 mph, he was too close to stop in time. He plowed into the rear of the car. Without his seat belt fastened, Tom was thrown forward against the steering wheel, crushing several ribs. Gas from the tank of the car in front burst into flames. The woman driver in front scrambled out safely. Tom, oblivious to the aching chest pain, focused only on Natalie. He unbuckled her seat belt (she wasn't allowed in the car without it), reached across her to open the passenger door, shoved her out, crawled out himself, grabbed Natalie, and, cradling her, rolled to the curb. He screamed at a passerby to summon an ambulance and directed the paramedics when they arrived.

Whichever form of shock — automatic pilot (like Tom) or immobilization (like Elizabeth and Shelley)— they are in, people can ignore their own injuries. Tom was aware of no pain as he moved to rescue Natalie. Others may take extraordinary action beyond ordinary capacity, like lifting the end of a car.

When the shock hits, still others may experience the auto pilot phase, even the prospect of their own death, as dispassionate observers.

"It was as if it was all happening in slow motion to someone else. I couldn't believe I was so unperturbed at that point."

"The van was now careening over the bridge, banging from one side rail to the other. After about the third bang — I think I banged them about five times— I realized that big semi-trailers come down that way, barreling down that hill over the bridge. It was at that point that I said to myself, quite calmly, 'OK, make peace with everybody, because you are going to die.'"

People not in the accident often make value judgments about how others handle themselves in crises like car accidents. The ironic fact is that many of one's actions are automatic and not at all considered or even conscious. Turn to Chapter Fourteen, "The Dumb Things People Say," for some vivid examples.

Control

One characteristic of any accident is that we — as human beings with our cherished illusion that we are in control — lose that control for some period.

As a species, human beings have thrived by taking control. We don't survive by modifying ourselves. We don't grow longer fur in the winter or change skin color to match the environment. We have thrived by growing bigger brains, figuring out how to modify the world around us, bending it to suit our needs. Therefore, when threatened and feeling out of sorts, we most often fall back on taking control, modifying things on our terms. So, after accidents, people pursue control, whether practical or illusory.

On the emergency room table, Dr. Tom angrily directed the emergency physician and the nurses through every step, cautioning against every possible oversight or miscue. The nurses were only too glad to give him the anesthetic and see him go to sleep for a time.

As a species, human beings have thrived by taking control.

Tom, effective at the scene of the accident while he was on auto pilot, was still in shock at the hospital. But now his actions in trying to reestablish control were at odds with the staff. Relinquishing control meant recognizing his vulnerability, but maintaining the illusion of control complicated everyone else's tasks.

As soon as people are out of control, they rush to gather control back. Some rush for control is practical and even heroic, like Tom rescuing Natalie. Other actions may seem inappropriate to an observer who wasn't in the accident.

Often, traffic officers sent to the scene of an accident will find bizarre behavior. A woman with a broken arm will try to put the groceries back in paper bags instead of tending to her arm. A man, just in an accident, will wander out onto the highway, dodging traffic, to retrieve a hubcap that rolled off the car. The police scratch their heads in bemusement as the motorist starts to put the hubcap back on a car that any other person can see is now a total wreck. Such actions don't make sense until we realize that the accident survivor is in shock and trying to reestablish control in whatever small way they can.

Control and powerlessness play a continuing role in car accident stress reactions, as you will find in Chapter Ten on page 65.

How Long Will It Last?

The period of shock will continue until the adrenaline wears off and the impact stage of digestion begins to set in. But if a crisis atmosphere remains, adrenaline may continue to flow for some time, prolonging the period of shock and auto pilot and postponing the time to deal with the impact of what has happened. If there are injuries, the impact may be postponed even longer, as the body adjusts.

SUMMARY

The first reactions of the car accident survivor are emergency reactions — outcry, shock, auto pilot, and control. Adrenaline prepares you for "fight or flight." Your reactions are not what they would be at other times.

[2] Carter, Shelley. "Rain, terror and a drunk driver on a dark road." *Cleveland Plain Dealer*, August 7, 1993.

[3] Carter, Shelley. As above.

CHAPTER

7

Finding Out About It:
First Reactions of the
Concerned Other

Outcry

For those who were not there, outcry and shock come at the instant you recognize that something awful has occurred and you are powerless to change it.

Finding Out About It

Megan's story began the book. Now listen to it from her father's point of view.

"It was a Sunday morning, and I was just finishing making breakfast for the kids. Megan was going off to work. I just happened to say to Megan, 'OK, you're running a little bit late — you're two minutes late. Make sure you're two minutes late when you get there. Don't rush.'

"She said, 'Sure, Dad!' And she took off.

"A little while later I hear sirens going by the house. Because it was fire trucks, my first reaction was that I should call my neighbor who lives down that end of the street and see if he was OK.

"And then, I heard police cars coming by . . . and then, emergency vehicles. Somebody who knows me pulled in the

No matter how much you have tried to prepare yourself for such a day, the impact when it actually happens is awful.

driveway and said, 'Megan's OK. We just went by there, and she's standing up.' Right then, I received a phone call from Megan saying, 'Dad, there has been a terrible accident, but I'm all right.'

"As I rushed out of the house, the people in the driveway told me, 'Relax.'

"I felt I was about to collapse. I didn't know what to do or say or anything. I don't know how I reacted to these people except that I was just running and jumping into my car and going. Suddenly I realized one of Megan's friends was there by herself. I was confused. I told her, 'Please stay here until I get back.' I rushed down to the corner, less than a quarter mile away.

"The police had the road blocked off. All I could see was the bottom of the car. My heart sank. I felt like collapsing when I didn't see Megan. Suddenly, she appeared from behind a policeman, and came running over and hugged me. Then I felt a lot better.

"Even though I had heard she was OK, I couldn't believe it until I saw she was OK."

The most important thing to recognize is that even if you were not in the accident, you are also very much affected by it. All the outcry, shock, and auto pilot that we noticed in the survivor will well up in you too.

You will have your own set of stress reactions that will mirror the process that your loved one is going through. And your reactions, like those of Megan's father, may be even more intense since you may be more quickly aware of the implications of all that has happened . . . and what more could go wrong. You won't have the advantage of shifting as readily into automatic pilot when you find out about it.

Others, too, have trouble believing what their eyes see and their mind knows.

Bruce and his wife, Jane, had been on a camping trip to the beach with friends. Jane left in her friend Lynn's car. Bruce and his friend, Dick, left a few minutes later in Dick's pickup truck.

"Dick and I were talking, and you could see up in the distance there had been an accident. I just had this notion that it was Lynn's car. And I kept telling myself, 'It can't be Lynn's because Lynn's isn't bent like that.' And Dick is talking, but I can't keep my eyes off what's up there.

"It was as if there was a hook on a fish line in my mouth or something. It jerked my head around and I see Lynn's car . . . But it can't be Lynn's car because it was completely destroyed. And I said to Dick, 'Dick, that's Lynn's car.' So we immediately pull over, we stop, we get out of the car.

"And I said to Dick, 'I can't go look, Dick. You have to go across and look and tell me if it's them.' I'm watching Dick as he walks over. He turns and looks at me with this terrible, confused and pained look on his face. I can't really remember anything after that for the next minute or two.

"The next thing I know I'm kneeling down next to Jane. She's lying there on the pavement and there are people around her — paramedics. She's shivering and I take her hand and I can see that she didn't go through the windshield or anything, she's alive!"

When the call comes or someone appears at the front door to tell you about your loved one's accident, your mind shuts down like Bruce's, and you have trouble absorbing the news.

"My mind went blank."

"Can this be happening to me?"

No matter how much you have tried to prepare yourself for such a day, rehearsed how you will react, and played out in

Even if you were not in the accident, you are also very much affected by it.

your mind the sinking feeling of hearing something like this, the impact when it actually happens is awful. The "Oh, my God!" may be quickly followed by a jumble of thoughts about what it means.

Recognition is followed by shock and numbing as you struggle to absorb the news.

"I felt drained. Everything went out of me.

"I thought, 'What will I do?' I just went and sat in my favorite green chair in the living room."

Your mind needs to take some time out. The familiar, such as the green chair, helps anchor you in this difficult time.

Your mind needs to take some time out. The familiar helps anchor you in this difficult time.

SUMMARY

Concerned others also have powerful first reactions when they find out about the accident. Not all of it will sink in at first. Even those not at the accident need time to react and adjust.

PHASE TWO:
DIGESTION

CHAPTER

8

The Impact Sets In

"It doesn't hit you for a while."

"I suddenly realized . . . "

Some time later, the impact of what has happened and its consequences begin to set in . . . and expand.

"All our plans for the future were gone . . . I realized I was going to be alone for the rest of my life!"

A few minutes, a few hours, a few days, a few months, a couple of years — the precise time for each of us will vary. As the shock wears off, the immediate danger is past and the crisis atmosphere subsides . . . then the impact of the accident sets in. *The phase of digesting the accident begins.*

Now you start absorbing exactly what happened and what it means.

Usually, people find that the impact begins to hit 4 to 48 hours after the accident. Whenever it starts, the full impact will gradually dawn on you in stages. If you had a high Stress Bill score, it will take months and sometimes years for it to fully settle in . . . and to settle out.

Many people cope well during the actual crisis itself. There are things to do to keep you focused and going. When the pressure is off, the reactions set in.

"I'm great in a crisis; I take care of business. It's only when it's all over that I fall apart."

When the pressure is off, the reactions set in.

"It never hit me 'till I got home and popped open a beer, then wham!"

The shift from emergency reactions to the digestion phase begins as the thoughts of what it all means suddenly rush in.

"I could be dead right now!"

"I might never walk again."

"I'll never see her or hold her again."

You start to recalculate the future with new information based on the accident. The greater the impact of the accident and its meaning on your life, the more time the recalculation will take. And the more you will have to pace yourself.

The Heart of Car Accident Stress

At the same time, as the thoughts of the new reality rush in, you also try to keep that full reality out of your mind. That produces the fundamental tension of all stress reactions — pulls in two directions.

"I'm trying to get it out of my mind for right now."

"Got to figure out what I need to do to get back in my normal style of life."

These two processes — realizing what really did happen, making sense of that new reality (and all that it means) . . . while also trying to get back to normal, the "old" normal, the way it was (or the way part of us says it should be) — are the major tensions of adjustment during the entire digestion phase.

The key to understanding car accident stress is recognizing the two opposite pulls on you as the digestion phase sets in.

Reflection and Distraction

From the time the impact begins to set in, nearly everything that happens will reveal a bouncing back and forth between some form of reflection on the accident and the new reality it has imposed on you . . . matched by an equally powerful force of distraction from that same reality.

By reflection, I mean some form of thinking about the accident and its ripples, trying to figure it all out, get it straight in your mind. By distraction, I mean some way of getting away from both the accident and the turmoil of reflecting on it. These two processes will be in constant tension throughout the rest of your recovery. That tension is at the heart of all car accident stress.

This digestion process of reflection and distraction happens after every accident, even a near miss or a fender bender. How long the process will take, and how painful it will be, is determined by how much change and new "reality" you have to digest. If the accident is minor, the process can be over in a few hours. The bigger the accident (and the Stress Bill), the more powerful the tension between reflection and distraction, and the longer time it will take to digest.

How Do Stress Reactions Work?

As you digest what has occurred, you experience phases of intense remembering mixed with periods of deliberately distracting activities. Small things remind you of the accident (or what might have been). And simultaneously, you get busy with other things so you don't have to think or remember. Tears come at the thought of what happened, and at that same moment, you want to deny it ever took place. If it was a very serious accident, you try to strike bargains with God. You alternate between feeling flooded with the realization of what has happened and having a desire to close it off, to deny the painful reality. Bouncing through this Ping-Pong trip is exhausting.

Why Do We Do This?

Our minds are wonderful. From the time we are infants,

These two tasks — realizing what really did happen, making sense of that new reality, and meanwhile also trying to get back to normal — are at the core of the adjustment process.

our eyes, ears, and mind carefully organize the world around what we have to deal with.

Think of where you are sitting right now reading. You probably have not been worried about whether a rock will smash the window near you or the light bulb in the lamp next to you will explode. By years of experience, you have learned what to assume and what to expect. Your mind pays attention to only the most important worries. Other possibilities are kept in storage. So when you are driving, your mind economically assumes that people will halt for a stop sign, that a pickup truck will not come at you down your side of the freeway, that you will arrive at your destination intact.

When an accident happens, it shatters some or many of those assumptions, the framework of your world. The unexpected did happen this time. Now you have to understand how it happened, why it happened, if it will happen again, and how it will affect your life from now on. Now your attention will have to be devoted to putting the pieces back together again.

Your mind is like a giant mapping program with millions of bits of information about your world. You spent your life growing up, building up a system map of how everything is supposed to work. Now you have to recalculate to take in the new data from the accident. The world and your life are no longer the way you thought and hoped they were. Now your body and your mind give you hints that the dials are spinning, and your mind is humming furiously. It is not a sign that you are going crazy. It is just evidence that a "system recalculation" is going on.

Hal had only a minor accident. But he still had to go through a recalculation process.

Hal had the green light. He thought, "Boy, I don't have to wait at all this time," and zoomed through. Off to his left, he caught a glimpse of the car coming at him. He had just enough time to turn the wheel slightly and say, "Oh, damn," to himself before the car slammed into him.

After the accident, at first he was very anxious every time he went through a green light. He startled at things, worried that he would be hit again. Gradually, he came to realize that, most times, he would not be hit. But, even months later, there was always a little twinge every time he went through. No longer innocent, but less anxious, he is sure to look quickly right and left every time.

Even minor accidents generate reactions and take time for adjustment. You wouldn't choose to spend time recalculating this way. And your mind naturally paces the impact as it sets in. It does this by moving you back and forth between recalculation and distraction, giving you some rest and some time out.

SUMMARY

After the emergency is over, the impact sets in. You try to piece together the puzzle of the accident and, at the same time, your mind tries to get away from that work. Going back and forth between figuring it out and getting away is the business of digestion . . . and of healing.

Reflection and Replay

As the impact hits and the digestion phase continues to set in, the reflection side of the equation will feel like it dominates. Reflection is the process of replaying the tape, taking in the new reality after the accident, then adjusting your assumptions and your outlook on the world. The new framework has to reflect the reality: the injuries, the expectations, and the losses — all the changes that the accident demands.

It is neither smooth nor easy. Let's look first at how reflection plays out in the digestion process. At first, it is very direct, re-experiencing the accident by replaying it. Later, you tie up the loose ends, make connections and "figure it out" in reflection that is less obvious.

Replaying It Over and Over

"The first few nights were really kind of scary. As soon as the lights went out, you really relived everything that had happened early that morning. You saw the lights coming, you heard the loud noise, felt the crash, and heard the screaming and hollering. It was really shaky."

Without wanting to do so and despite all your best efforts to distract yourself, your mind replays parts of the accident. You play "what if" and "if only" . . . what could have prevented it. You try to figure out what happened, why and who is to blame. It's a way of restoring order to a world turned upside down.

"The accident happened just a few weeks ago, and it still replays over and over in my mind, and every time the memory picture flickers on, I flinch again."

"The accident happened just a few weeks ago, and it still replays over and over in my mind, and every time the memory picture flickers on, I flinch again." [4]

"I keep thinking about it. Trying to figure out what really did happen."

"Why did it happen?"

Clinicians talk about these as intrusive thoughts — they barge into our minds and force their way into our consciousness. The most unexpected things can trigger them.

Triggering Events

"Little things would remind me of it and bring all the memories rushing back."

You find yourself shuttling back and forth between the normal, the routine, and the replay.

"I hear a brake squeal or a car backfire and it all comes back. I see a red Ford like mine and I can't tell if I'm here or there. I have to look around and check."

"I thought I was fine again and then I came across his leather gloves sitting on the hall table. I realized he was gone and I burst into tears."

No matter how well you close it off, or think you have it under control, little things will bring it all flooding back to remind you of what it means. A form comes from the insurance company . . . One question on the accident report hits you the wrong way . . . The family pictures you had taken six months ago finally arrive . . . Your car registration comes in the mail . . . And the full impact hits — again — and you feel overwhelmed.

Let's look next at how the accident plays out in other types of reflection.

"I hear a brake squeal or a car backfire and it all comes back."

Dreams and Nightmares

"I've had only one or two good nights of sleep since the accident. The bad dreams keep coming back."

People often have dreams or nightmares in which they play out the events of the accident over and over. I find it most useful to regard these as signals of the unfinished business that we haven't resolved within ourselves about the accident.

The nightmares bring back to us precisely those aspects that remain unresolved.

"There I was in the hospital kicking up a real fuss. What I didn't tell them was that I was having these nightmares. I kept seeing my mother sitting in the front seat, stone still. I would see the wave of water from the road wash over the car. I could feel the car begin to spin. Then I would have these images of the truck looming in front of us, the sudden stop, and then Mom floating forward toward the windshield. I'd want to reach out and stop it but I didn't know what to do. I knew if I told the doctors they'd blame me for killing her."

Often in dreams you tell yourself the awful "truths" you automatically hide from yourself in your waking hours. That doesn't make the dreams "true," but they are keys to your secret thoughts. The best way to handle these dreams is to allow yourself to make them conscious and confront the unresolved business and clarify the "truths." This is easier in the telling than in the doing, but later in the chapter you will see how you can manage the dreams and nightmares.

Sleep Disruptions

Not all the sleep problems stem from nightmares. Often people find themselves waking up in a cold sweat in the middle of the night without being aware of what woke them up. The sheets are twisted around them, and they realize they've been thrashing about. But upon awakening, they are not conscious

Often in dreams you tell yourself the awful "truths" you automatically hide from yourself in your waking hours.

of any dreams. Sometimes the unfinished business is so painful that our minds won't even face it directly in sleep. These disruptions generally happen in the middle of the night rather than just before waking in the morning.

Some people will often consciously avoid going to sleep in order to avoid the nightmares and dreams. Some plan their sleep habits around the nightmares, waking up at 2 a.m. to watch TV and avoid the dreams — good examples of homemade distraction from the demands of reflection.

Startle Reactions

Billy was hit by a car that ran through a stop sign and hit him broadside. He had watched it coming, sure that the other driver knew he was there and would stop. Now, on his way to work, he can't avoid that same four-way stop intersection. One time, shortly after the accident, another car started through the intersection at the same time Billy did and blew his horn. Billy found himself frozen at the wheel, unable to move. He noticed he was trembling from head to toe, and his heart was beating so fast he thought it would jump out of his chest.

Startle reactions are signs our bodies are reacting as if the accident were happening all over again. It is the mind's preparation for another "flight or fight" moment. And people like Billy find themselves frozen — suspended for the moment — trying to figure out what is real.

So much of what we do is automatic. We assume that cars will stop for the red light and not crash into us. What happens when those assumptions are violated profoundly shakes us up.

Let's think about it in another way for a moment. As you read, have you thought about the ceiling collapsing on you and the roof falling in? You have good reason to assume that the floor under you will hold the weight of you and the chair you are in. Though hers isn't a car accident, let Cindy demonstrate what happens when those assumptions get violated.

Cindy lived in an apartment complex where a gas leak in the basement laundry room was ignited early one morning. The building exploded. The roof and floors collapsed. Several weeks later, Cindy was back at work and living in a new apartment. Listen to what she said about hearing people walk in the apartment above.

"I'm living downstairs now in an apartment complex. And I hear people walking above me and I watch the walls."

Cindy dashes over and checks the walls to make sure they are not falling in. She has to reason with herself that the explosion is not happening again even though her body keeps reacting to sounds as if it were.

Cindy lost her innocence about accidents and now has to find a new set of rules. The assumptions that "innocent" people live under cannot be restored. Framing new rules takes time and a renewed experience of safety.

Flashbacks

In a flashback, memories are recalled so vividly that you almost feel as if you are actually reliving the moment. Flashbacks are usually triggered by a sound or smell that casts you vividly back into the event. Most often, part of you knows that it is not real, but the memory is so vivid it feels like you are reliving the event again — in Technicolor.

Adele is driving in a hard rain on the freeway. It nearly undoes her. The smell and sound of the rain on the car propel the memories, both of the skid and of the eerie stillness of her mother's body after the crash, freshly into her mind. It's as if she is right back there. Suddenly she can't tell if the tires now are holding or she is skidding. She thinks she is losing her grip. Though at some level she knows she is OK, she has to pull over and coax herself back into the present.

Part of you knows that it is not real, but the memory is so vivid it feels like you are reliving the event again — in Technicolor.

Sometimes the flashback is a mere hint.

Larry was nearly killed in a bad wreck. When he finally was back driving, something would happen in traffic and a shudder like a bolt of lightning would pass through his vision and his body.

What to Do — About Sleep Disruptions And Nightmares

You don't have to just suffer. You can modify your patterns. Find out what works for you.

Change when you sleep
Andrea found herself unable to sleep or wracked by nightmares and panic attacks when she was alone at night. Her husband worked the night shift. She began staying up reading and watching TV at night and sleeping during the day when her husband was home and she felt safe.

It's not forever, and you can go back to your usual patterns when the dreams ease.

Make the replay productive
Some of the events will recur in thoughts, reminders, or dreams. Especially at first, you cannot control the time, the place, or the triggers. You are in a process, and you can't wrench your mind back to where it was before the accident. But you can let go and, by recognizing the process, guide yourself through it.

The thoughts that keep popping into your head are a sign of your mind pressing you to figure out what hap-

---

pened (and what it means). Here's how to make that time work for you instead of against you.

Choose an ally

Choose the person that you want to talk with . . . someone you really trust. You may already know who the ideal person is. If not, think of the people you know who have faced a real crisis. Are there some you respect for the way they handled it? If so, ask them to be your guide. Ask them not to try to protect you or give you answers but simply to listen. Tell them you need help to talk to yourself. When you are ready, ask them how they got through the replay.

Set a specific time

Set aside a specific time to talk (or think) about what happened and what it means. Pick the time of the day or week when you feel most comfortable (or least uncomfortable) talking about the accident. Then use that time to talk and think it through.

Pick a safe place

Choose a comfortable spot where you feel safe and won't be disturbed. Then snuggle in and hug a cushion.

Don't fight it

Instead of resisting, give yourself permission, in those moments, to not be in control and to not understand it all. Relax and let the memories and thoughts come. As you let yourself react and then listen to yourself, the answers within you will emerge.

Don't stuff it

Don't sabotage the process by covering up your mood with drugs, alcohol, or food. This is a time to heal.

Remind yourself that it is a memory

When you find yourself startled again, replaying the accident, or feeling as if the accident were happening all over, pause, take a deep breath and tell yourself, "It is not happening again. It's over and I survived. I'm safe and it's OK. These are just painful memories." Remember that reflecting on and working through your memories is what is healing.

Expect a reaction

The memories and thoughts are connected to feelings. They can seem as intense as the accident itself. Let them flow for the time you have allowed. Healing the spirit is like healing the body . . . it is both painful and exhausting. And it takes time.

Give yourself a time limit

"I'll run this through for half an hour. But I don't have to solve it all today; I'll see it differently tomorrow."

Then set another time to do more. You don't have to come up with all the answers today.

When you can't control the replay time

If the memories come and you have not had the chance to set a time with an ally, share the dreams or memories with someone else. Get through it. Talk to yourself. Then find a way to let your ally (or someone else) know what happened. Pick people to talk with whom you can trust to just listen, rather than to overreact or to try to fix it for you. Don't keep the memories inside. They're corrosive.

Nurture yourself

Have a cup of tea. Give yourself a treat. Take a break and do something special. You need it and you deserve it.

Take a break

Instead of resisting, learn how to plan times when it's OK to really think about these things . . . and then take a break until that time.

When you have chosen the time to listen to your reactions and have created a safe situation to do that, give yourself permission to put off until the allotted time the disturbing thoughts that pop in your mind. When the thoughts creep in, recognize them and tell yourself that it's OK, "I'm going to deal with these things tomorrow when I talk with X. I've already set that up, and right now I don't have to think about it."

All these are forms of reflection — absorbing the reality. Throughout the process of recovery, you will find bits of the reality presenting themselves to be absorbed. The reflection process will not be so disruptive forever if you make it productive. But some form of reflection will continue until you have reached resolution — acceptance of the full reality. Meanwhile, you will find that reflection and digestion of the new reality are constantly tempered by various stages of distraction.

SUMMARY

The most powerful form of reaction to an accident is reflection. It means replaying the accident in your mind, dreaming about it, figuring it out in a number of ways. The first thing that helps is simply understanding how this reflection and replay work. The second tool is managing the replay process and making it work for your recovery.

[4] Carter, Shelley. "Rain, terror and a drunk driver on a dark road." *Cleveland Plain Dealer*, August 7, 1993.

10

Distraction and More Digestion

As replay and the other forms of reflection tug at you in the digestion phase, an opposite pull exerts its force — distraction. Distraction is the effort to get away from the jarring realities imposed by the accident and its ramifications . . . to block those realities out, deny them, get back to the world you knew before the accident . . . and pretend that it never happened or wasn't as bad as it was.

There are several ways you distract yourself following a car accident. How blatant they are will depend on the size of your Stress Bill.

Denial and Disbelief

"There must be some mistake! He was just running on those legs yesterday."

"Maybe he'll make it . . ."

"She's just resting. She'll wake up."

The first and most common distraction is denial of the news and its reality.

"I can't believe it happened. I keep closing my eyes and thinking when I open them everything will be all right."

Your mind can't take it all in at once. The accident and its ramifications have to be filtered in . . . slowly, one drop at a

> **Distraction is the effort to get away from the realities imposed by the accident . . . to block them out, deny them, get back to the reality you knew before the accident . . . and pretend that it never happened or wasn't as bad as it was.**

time. Denial and disbelief are the crude first line of defense as your mind marshals its resources. How much you have to block out is a measure of how much of a challenge your mind knows it has to handle.

Though denial is very evident in the early stages of shock and impact, you will find yourself using it again and again throughout the Digestion Phase. Sometimes it will make you smile at how vigorous and constant a force it remains.

Getting Away from It

As the impact is felt, you find yourself exhausted and spent. The changes and challenges you face are enormous. You need a break. In the Digestion Phase, you get that break from reflection and replay by trying to forget about it for a time.

"I cleaned and I scrubbed . . . anything to keep from thinking."

Just as you were compelled to replay the accident and at first found yourself talking about it constantly, you also feel a need to control the replay and talk. One way is to get back into a routine. Reading the quote about cleaning, some people mentioned how they used cleaning and scrubbing as a familiar routine to think about what they faced. It helped them feel in control. The familiar is a great comfort in this time of strain. That is the sign of a healthy mind at work, pacing the recovery.

As people try to get back into a routine, the accident is something they don't like to talk about. One college student in a school bus accident commented:

"You meet people who were there in the accident, but they don't want to talk about it. You see them on campus sometimes, but people are trying to forget it, trying to get it out of their minds for right now."

You do not have a choice about whether you are going to go through this recovery process. Your only option is to choose how you are going to manage it. And finding ways to pace yourself is a major step.

In the previous chapter, we discussed the issue of talking about it. But you will find yourself of two minds. On the one hand, you don't want to talk about the accident. On the other hand, you will find you can't stop talking and thinking about it.

As you first bounce among feelings of sadness, anger, self-pity, blame, and bitterness, you try to cut those feelings off.

"As soon as something started to bubble up, I'd quickly find something to take my mind off it."

The impact of the accident will not hit you all at once. Your mind tempers the process as it sets in over time. The gift you give yourself is the allowance you make for pacing yourself . . . making time for reflection and for distraction. The harm comes when you do not understand and respect your recovery, and instead try to rush, short cut, or deny the process.

Control, Powerlessness, and Lack of Control

Denial and disbelief are fairly blunt forms of distraction. They are the first line of defense against the reality of the accident. Another closely related and powerful form of distraction is control. The ramifications of the accident can seem overwhelming as the shock begins to wear off. We talked about how comforting the familiar is. One way of coping with the powerlessness and lack of control you suddenly are faced with is to grab fierce control of those things you can be in charge of.

Donna was on her way home over Donner Pass to Lake Tahoe, driving her favorite red convertible sports car. Suddenly, a huge elk appeared in front of her and then charged at her car. He struck the left front of the fiberglass car body. In a flash, he was on the hood, then completely covered the windshield and just as quickly was flying over her head and vanished . . . all in a matter of seconds.

> **The familiar is a great comfort in this time of strain. That is the sign of a healthy mind at work, pacing the recovery.**

The flip side of seemingly pointless attempts to regain control is the feeling of being out of control and unable to restore order to our world.

The car wobbled as she struggled to regain control. She continued driving for a minute and then realized she was trembling badly. She stopped for a moment, and got out to gather herself when she realized her legs and bare feet were covered with thousands of beads of glass from her shattered windshield.

She drove on slowly into the town at the base of the mountain and stopped at a repair station. Donna told them she was hit by a deer. The mechanic laughed and said, "No. I'm a hunter. That's elk fur on your car." Donna asked about replacing the shattered windshield. There was no stock in town and she was told she would have to wait two days for delivery. Donna burst into tears. "I'm only 75 minutes away over Donner Pass; I want to go home."

Donna suddenly began to feel out of control. She felt at the mercy now of complications from the accident. So she found a way to reassert some control.

Determined not to cry and to be strong, she fought back the tears and asked, "Why can't I just drive the car back?" "Because the windshield is shattered and your face is going to be pelted by flying glass all the way, lady," came the answer.

"Forget it," Donna said to herself. Slipping on a scarf, a hat, and her fancy new wraparound sunglasses, Donna climbed back in the car. Glass beads flew back at her, bouncing off the sunglasses as she drove over the pass and home.

Donna had taken control, and God help anyone who had tried to detain her. But once she got home other things became apparent.

Donna's friends realized the car was wrecked. People pointed out glass beads in her hair and on her face, and nicks in her sunglasses. As friends gathered, they kidded her that she had an elk mobile, noting how the car was almost covered in elk fur. It looked fur lined.

Notice the uncomfortable edge in her friends' reactions and comments. You will find more on this in Chapter Fourteen, "The Dumb Things People Say."

Donna herself realized she had never noticed any of it and had felt nothing. Her determined control had helped her block out the reality of her fears and upset until she could get to a safe place.

Notice how Donna fought off the tears and panic of being at loose ends for two days away from home by taking control and driving home through the glass shower. The fear, the danger, her powerlessness over the car, and the required wait for the windshield — all were tucked away until she got over the pass and home. Only then would she let the reality sink in.

"I was overwhelmed with feelings of fear. Would I get hit again? Would I ever be safe in a car again?"

People often feel out of control after an accident. The flip side of seemingly pointless attempts to regain control (like chasing the hubcaps on page 39) is the feeling of being out of control and unable to restore order to our world. Donna delayed the feeling of being out of control by driving home with the shattered windshield.

"I can't get it fixed, so I'll just drive home."

Such direct action may seem practical, fearless, pointless, or even reckless to others. That is not the point. The behavior — whatever its practical or foolish purpose — is a direct manifestation of the conflict over powerlessness and control and a wonderful form of temporary distraction from the full reality of what has happened. Such action thus can serve several purposes, practical and psychological.

After an accident, intense clinging to control over unrelated things or panic at the thought of being out of control are common illustrations of this form of distraction. What confuses others is that the occasion that raises the control issue may not seem directly connected to the accident. So when someone fights fiercely over the grocery list or what checks to write, it often has more to do with the accident and control than with the list or the money.

Further Stages of Digestion

There are several other subtle forms that distraction will take — the more sophisticated forms which offer distraction and temper reflection.

Now, as you move through your recovery, you will notice other stages[5] of the digestion process that usually involve elements of both reflection and distraction — both figuring it out and getting away from the realities and the implications of the accident . . . flip sides of digesting it. In each successive stage of digestion, you move gradually closer to absorbing the reality, accepting and moving on.

Bargaining with God

One wonderful stage of digestion that involves both coming to terms with and warding off the reality of the accident is bargaining with God. Your mind knows the enormity of what has happened, but the very power of the accident and its consequences threaten to overwhelm you. You attempt to mitigate the impact of that realization by clutching at straws, striking a hurried bargain, anything to hold off what you know in your heart is now true.

"If you let my son walk again, I'll give 10 percent of my income in contributions."

Sometimes you think to yourself, "Am I going crazy?" No, you are not going crazy. But you are reacting. No one is immune.

The implications, the changes and what they mean, begin to set in. Your mind works with blinding speed. You catch a momentary glimpse of the implications and threats of the accident — quickly look around for an escape to close it all off — know somehow it is real and can't just be denied — and so decide to reduce the consequences by striking a bargain.

"What If . . . " and "If only . . . "

"What if" and "If only" are two special forms of digestion. They are critical to the recovery process because they allow you to sip some of the reality while trying out other outcomes. Like the tenderness around a wound, they are among the most painful parts of the healing process, too.

Philip was driving along a country road on his way to play golf. A young mother with her small child was driving a van heading in the opposite direction. As she passed by him going over a rise, the van slid on the wet pavement. Philip never noticed her. The van slid across the center stripe and clipped his rear end. It spun him around and sent him through the ditch and into the woods.

It all happened so quickly that he didn't know what had happened. But none of the three were injured.

Only after he got out of his wrecked car and saw the cliff down to the river only 30 feet behind him did he suddenly realize how bad it could have been. "What if it had happened a few feet sooner? I would have gone off the cliff into the river. I'd be dead."

The realization of what might have happened dawned on Philip, and his mind raced to the scenarios of what might have been.

On Philip's Stress Bill scale, his was a minor accident. No one was hurt. Even so, for a time he racked his brain . . . considering the accident and what led up to it, from every angle . . . trying to find a way to make sure it came out "right."

When it is more serious, you want to make it come out dif-

> "If only I'll be OK again, I'll go to church every Sunday."

> He racked his brain . . . considering the accident and what led up to it, from every angle . . . trying to find a way to make it came out "right."

ferently. Adele, whose 80-year-old mother was killed when Adele skidded in the rain on the freeway, had a difficult time with the "if onlys" while she lay in the hospital recovering.

"If only I hadn't driven back in the rain that night, my mother would be alive. What if we had stopped for dinner and waited out the heaviest part, she might . . ."

Reevaluation

These reconsiderations often lead you to reflect on other parts of your life and wonder what you are doing and why.

Julie is a psychiatrist who works with rape victims. She and her husband left summer camp in Maine, where they had gone to pick up their daughter and her friend at the end of camp. Julie and her family set out early in the morning to avoid traffic. In the fog, Julie saw a deer dash from the side of the road directly in front of her. She swerved to avoid hitting the deer.

Swinging the wheel back sharply, Julie put the car into a roll. As the car began to tumble, she had images of the teenagers in the back seat being bounced off the roof and the walls of the car. Fortunately, Julie and her husband were belted in and the kids had wedged themselves in with duffel bags and sleeping bags. Other than being shaken up, everyone was OK. The car was wrecked but the family managed to get home.

Julie found she was critical of herself, replaying — If only I had not left so early, the deer would not have been out. What if we had flown instead of driven? She found herself irritated at her husband, who had insisted that they drive rather than fly.

In the next two weeks she was haunted by dreams and nightmares of the crash. Julie found herself daydreaming in her office, wondering why she had given up teaching English literature and become a psychiatrist anyway. She found herself critical of her marriage, her job, and her life.

> **"If only I hadn't driven back in the rain that night, my mother would be alive. What if we had stopped for dinner and waited out the heaviest part, she might . . ."**

Even as an observer or outsider to the actual accident you may have your own set of "what ifs" and "if onlys" and find yourself reexamining your own set of personal responsibilities.

Irritability and Anger

After her accident, Barbara found she was irritable and short with her family.

"I yelled at my son for spilling the juice. I kept on finding myself being upset and picking on them for things I ordinarily just wouldn't react to."

Finding yourself short of temper, after the accident is very common. And the more lack of control you feel, the more irritable you will feel.

Sometimes the irritability, anger, and frustration that cannot yet find expression at the accident and those who caused it find ways for you to punish those you love.

"Last night I made my husband drive my [smashed] car. I wanted him to be in my shoes and know what it was like to have to get in on the passenger side, to feel the dent next to him, to know what it was like for me."

Finally, the anger will surface at those who you feel were responsible (or irresponsible).

"I was so angry I couldn't see straight. I'd done nothing to deserve it. I wanted to punch someone."

Anger is an important milestone in letting the reality sink in. The injustice, the unfairness, all prompt a return of feeling after a period of numbness.

"I know that the next five minutes, the next hour, hell, the

These reconsiderations often lead you to reflect on other parts of your life and wonder what you are doing and why.

Sometimes the
irritability, anger,
and frustration that
cannot yet find
expression at the
accident and those
who caused it find
ways for you to
punish those you
love.

next day, is not guaranteed to me or anybody else. I did not ask this man to drink and get behind the wheel and become a lethal weapon just to give me a reality check. He jeopardized my life. His total disregard for that child [in the car] with him, and for everybody else on the road that night, is intolerable."[6]

Anger is an important step. But people let it out differently. Not everyone is in touch with the anger at the same pace. For a dramatic example, read the section on emotional numbness in Chapter Eleven.

"It just wasn't fair. My car was hit from behind. He should never have been driving without brakes. I'm over the initial shock but not over the anger."

Anger also can arouse fears of what will happen if the anger gets out.

"I can't talk about it, or I'll get so angry I'll lose control."

Anger is powerful because it not only is legitimate but also can provide a channel for releasing other emotions you may not be aware of or have held in check. That adds to its power.

What to Do — About Anger

Accept it
It is a key to feelings. It's often the only one you have right now.

Don't hide it
Anger can spur you to action and lead to positive change. *Remember the difference between feeling the anger and expressing it.*

Don't feed on it

The fact that you feel anger doesn't mean you have to express it. It is not uncontrollable or violent in itself. It's a powerful force. Learn to direct it and ride it like a wild horse. Make anger work for you.

Channel anger constructively

Write a letter to the person you are angry with. You can decide later when and whether to send it.

Tell your story to the authorities

Agree to testify. If a law needs to be changed, talk to your legislators. But take care of yourself and your family too.

Blame

"He had had three drunk driving convictions before, and they never did anything but slap his wrist."

One major pitfall of stress reactions is the trap of blame. You feel out of control. You are angry and irritable. All of it is amplified after the accident. You think to yourself,

"Why do I have to go through all of this? It's not fair."

Blame can become an outlet for that frustration. You focus on what "they" did wrong. How stupid, inconsiderate, negligent, and even hostile it was. And it was. You are right. They should be held accountable for what happened. And there may be a part for you to play in that accountability.

The trap lies in letting that blame distract you from what is going on with you and the things you can control . . . but may be frightened of. Then blame helps shift the focus from pain.

Consider the remarks of the mother of a young girl who

Anger is an important milestone in letting the reality sink in.

survived an accident in which the girl's best friend died.

"It's hard to explain to [her]. I just told her the truth, that she's not welcome and couldn't go to [her friend's] funeral. I would like to have gone and paid my respects, and I would have gone. It would have been hard for me, but I would have liked to have gone. It's cruel, is what it is. It just boils down to the fact that one child died [in the accident] and one child survived. I just hate to have all the blame put on my family."[7]

Anger and blame are natural reactions. But if they don't find useful expression, they can linger corrosively.

Years later, Sarah is still troubled by one part of her reactions to her son's accident.

As a teenaged passenger, Jeremy had been badly injured in an accident in which one of his friends was killed. Sarah found herself carefully noting who among her "friends" called and went to visit him at the hospital. Sarah confessed that she had kept a mental list of everyone's behavior and added black marks for those who failed to measure up.

Recently [fifteen years after the accident], a friend called to ask for Jeremy's address in Seattle where he and his family now live. The friend's daughter and her family had just moved to Seattle and wanted to get in touch with Jeremy. Sarah declined to give the address.

What immediately flashed through her mind was an incident from the time of the accident. The friend called Sarah and asked if there was anything she and her daughter could do for Jeremy. Sarah suggested that Jeremy would really appreciate a visit from the friend's daughter. The friend thought about it and then declined, saying that the daughter didn't feel she knew Jeremy well enough. Sarah felt offended and never forgot.

Now, when faced with the request 15 years later for Jeremy's address, she refused, knowing in her heart that it was in retalia-

tion for what Sarah felt was the earlier snub.

Sarah confessed this tentatively to me, describing it as "mean-spiritedness." She was amazed at the demonstration of how capable she was of bitterness and small-mindedness.

Such a mixed reaction — a long-held grudge and a concern about how "mean-spirited" it feels — is not uncommon. It usually reflects some other reaction that has remained unresolved. I asked Sarah what she might be "holding on to." She immediately identified some guilt over other behavior. More details about her answer are found in the section on guilt in Chapter Twelve.

If you find that your focus is "out there" . . . and there are things you are neglecting in yourself or your loved ones . . . blame may have become a distraction for you, so you don't have to pay attention to "in here."

Finally, you are what you put out into the world. If you carry blame too long, it is not restricted to those who deserve it, and you end up laying it on all those close to you. Blame comes to define a major part of who you are. You have to make a choice — to heal or to let the bitterness corrode your life.

Repetition

The worst terror comes when accidents repeat themselves.

Paul's van was hit by an airplane. He worked at a major airport. While waiting to pick up a flight crew off a commuter flight, he was parked at the jetway. The new pilot had had a rough landing and misjudged the parking slot. The plane's propeller tore into Paul's van, shredding it and barely missing him.

A few weeks later, Paul was parked in the same slot about to go off duty. A fuel truck mistakenly backed into his new van, spilling jet fuel all around him. Miraculously, no fire ignited. But two weeks later, Paul found a way to leave the job. It had become too close for comfort.

"Why do I have to go through all of this? It's not fair."

Sometimes it is just bad luck. But stress reactions are a process of repetition.

"I don't think the feeling ever goes away. The fear. That unexpected feeling of fear. Even now, there are times when I'm on the freeway and it returns. It just comes up on me.

You can find yourself inadvertently recreating the circumstances over and over in a subconscious attempt to get it "right."

"Like a year ago, I was on the freeway driving and I had that feeling again, the thought about being rear-ended, the sound, the feeling of flying. And the next thing I know, the guy in front of me runs into the car in front of him. I don't know if I saw it coming or it was just a coincidence, but it really shook me up."[8]

All the repeated memories and thoughts are evidence of the digestion and recalculation going on following the accident. When that recalculation is blocked and important thoughts and memories are not actively reworked, they find an indirect or subconscious route to play out. You find yourself inadvertently recreating the circumstances over and over in a subconscious attempt to get it right.

Simon was a 55-year-old man who hated to walk all the way to the crosswalk down the street from his office. One morning on his way to court, thinking about other things, he crossed the street in the middle of the block. He forgot to check the traffic and was hit by a car. After recovering from the broken leg, he returned to work. "Never bothered me for a minute," he insisted. Three weeks later, he wandered out into the same busy traffic again and was killed.

Other times, unresolved reactions subconsciously guide later apprehensions.

Rita was riding in a convertible, which was hit head on. It was in the days before seat belts. She was catapulted out of the car and over the one that hit her. She landed on the roadway behind the other car. A teenager at the time, all she remembered was her father, a dentist, calling her in the hospital. The only thing he wanted to know was if she had lost any teeth. Being young, she put it all behind her.

Somehow, she has had eight minor accidents since then. She wonders why she is so anxious driving in rush hour. She drives a Volvo and her children tease her, telling her she's a menace on the road.

There is no free lunch. The bill gets paid directly or indirectly.

What I have illustrated here are the many direct and indirect forms that digestion may take as you absorb the experience by both reflecting and distracting yourself during these different stages.

SUMMARY

Whether by denial, disbelief, or control, you try to get away from the realities of the accident, put it out of your mind and get some relief . . . get back to "normal."

Then there are many other subtle forms that the digestion phase takes. Grasping for control, bargaining with God, the what ifs and if onlys, reevaluation, anger, irritability, blame, and repetition are all stages of absorbing the accident. The trap lies in getting stuck in one stage.

[5] Dr. Elisabeth Kübler-Ross explained these stages so well in her work with terminally ill patients described in her book, *On Death and Dying* (1969). Though she was dealing with death, we have come to find that the same stages mark all traumatic reactions.

[6] Carter, Shelley. "Rain, terror and a drunk driver on a dark road." *Cleveland Plain Dealer*, August 7, 1993.

[7] Harris, Rich (AP). *Cleveland Plain Dealer*, November 26, 1991, p. C1.

[8] Dawn Gregerson, Volvo ad, 1992.

11

Your "Package" and Other Signs of Your Stress Reactions

Just as the grocery bag on the front seat is thrown forward when you stop the car suddenly, you are cast by psychological momentum through a series of reactions to the accident. You may find yourself with dreams, nightmares, fears, anxieties, irritations, and distractions that you don't connect directly with the accident. In this chapter, we will talk about the signs that suggest you are experiencing natural reactions to the stress of the accident. Of course, few people have every one of these reactions. You will see your own reaction pattern. And you will learn that these reactions are a "package" deal. You don't get to select just the ones you want.

The signs of stress reactions are neither good nor bad. They just are. You are different than you were before the accident, and that is one source of your frustration. These symptoms are indications of the healing process at work.

You can either accept them as signs of where you are and make them tools of your progress, or you can fight them and try to bury them, hoping they will go away with time.

Time by itself doesn't heal stress. The work you do while time passes is what brings change. The bill still is due, even if you decide to defer it.

Your "Package"

If the basic process of stress is the tension between reflection

> **Feelings aren't the only reactions. You have a whole "package" of reactions... You can either treat them as signs of what is bubbling in you . . . or ignore them at your peril.**

Wanting to get rid of
your "package" is
like saying you don't
want the gas gauge
in your car because
it's reading empty.
You can block out
the gauge, but the
tank will still
run dry.

and distraction, then one of your tools for coping with the stress is knowing where and how these reactions are going to show up. We have just talked about some forms of replay and denial. However, car accident stress shows up in more subtle ways, which you may not connect directly to the accident.

Feelings aren't the only reactions. You have a whole "package"[9] of signs of your reactions. Some you may notice yourself, others may be more apparent to the people around you. You can either treat them as signs of what is bubbling in you . . . or ignore them at your peril.

Body

Your body will show some of the reactions you might not recognize otherwise. Tension, anxiety, strain, and exhaustion are all clues about the reactions and their toll.

Emotions

You may feel sad, depressed, angry, anxious, nervous, or excited. You will probably feel all these emotions at one time or another during your recovery.

Behavior

You find yourself unable to sleep. You notice you pace, eat, drink, and smoke more. Someone points out how short-tempered you get with others. These changes in behavior are signals of other reactions you may be ignoring.

Thoughts

Your thoughts related to the accident are an important sign of the process you are going through. They will pop into your head whether you want them to or not. They are the clues to what your mind is trying to figure out.

Associations

You will think of other people and situations. These associations are clues to the connections and meanings

There are subtle
ways in which
reactions show up
that you may not
connect directly to
the accident.

you are creating from the accident and its aftermath.

Memories

Memories and reminders will come to mind, no matter how hard you try to avoid them or attempt to keep them out. You may feel like you can't control them, but you can learn to manage them. Wanting to get rid of them is like saying you don't want the gas gauge in your car because it's reading empty. You can block out the gauge, but the tank will still run dry.

"Every time I come to an intersection, my stomach is in my mouth, my heart is pounding, I hold my breath."

The Signs of Stress Reactions

The signs of stress reactions follow the pattern of alternating phases of replaying the accident and putting off thinking about it. Very often, one symptom will be matched by another one that reflects the mirror opposite of the first.

For example, people frequently find that they are distracted and forgetful. They think there is something wrong with their memory. Yet, at the same time, they find themselves bombarded with vivid memories and images from the accident. Neither sign is the whole truth. Taken together, the seemingly contradictory symptoms flesh out a fuller picture of the back-and-forth tasks of the recovery process.

You may notice that you swing between the symptoms of reflection and distraction several times a day, even minute to minute. One minute you feel guilty about an "if only," and the next you are enraged, cursing the drunk driver who hit you. These swings, as you work through the process, are what make it so exhausting. The good news is that the swings get less frequent as you complete the digestion process.

Fears and Anxieties

Fears and anxieties are common after an accident. They range from the specific to the general.

"Little things that never bothered me set off waves of fear these days. I was even frightened of the washing machine."

"I seem to be anxious all the time now."

Many people notice a general sense of anxiety and foreboding — something bad is going to happen — for a time after the accident.

Others find they have specific fears. Some are related directly to the accident.

"I had been trapped in my car after the accident. They had to cut me out. Now even when I ride the subway I find that I get claustrophobic. My stomach is tight and I'm looking around for how to get out."

Other fears seem unrelated to the accident. You may feel a shiver of fear that your apartment has been broken into every time you open the front door. Or, for no good reason, you may suddenly feel that your job is on the line.

Fear of Repetition

"It may be tomorrow night or it may be next year. I live in fear that it will happen again."

"Every time I come to an intersection, my stomach is in my mouth, my heart is pounding, I hold my breath. Automatically my foot is pressing the brake into the floor. I wait and look around expecting that someone else will slam into me and it will happen all over again."

These are fears directly connected to terror that the accident will happen again. Your innocence has given way to a new vulnerability.

"I don't think people really see a car for what it is. It's something we use every day, but it's something that can kill you. Or save you."[10]

Other fears are generated by anticipation.

"What will it be like when I have to ride in a car again?"

"Will I ever be able to drive again?"

"I know that's how he drives, but now it really gets to me."

Avoidance Activities

One common strategy people turn to as a way of coping with the fears is to restrict their activities.

"I just won't drive for a while."

"I wouldn't get into a car for several weeks."

Another more subtle form of coping with anxieties and fears is to modify your behavior patterns. Listen to this truck driver who was nearly knocked off the road by a dropped load of concrete pipe.

"They couldn't ever move those pipes. So for years they have lain next to the highway there, overgrown with weeds. Every time I would drive by, I would shudder.

"My boss started to get irritated with me because I kept being late for work. I couldn't figure it out until someone who rode with me pointed out that I was driving to work by this long out-of-the-way route. I realized I had secretly vowed never to go near that intersection again."

What to Do — About Fears and Anxieties

1. Look at your fear and face it
Name your fears. Make a list of exactly what you fear most. It reduces the anxiety. Only you have to see the list. So don't be concerned about how trivial or extreme or silly you think others might feel it is. List anything

---

that worries you. Be specific. What are you afraid will happen? When?

Then think about how can you make life a little safer right now. What would help? Do that for right now. You can change your behavior later.

2. Take a deep breath
Try breathing exercises.

3. Take your time
Wait until you are ready. Make a choice about whether you have to face each thing now or want to do it on your timetable.

4. Practice what you are going to face
Imagine it. Walk through the steps that are scary before you actually do them. Plan how you want to respond to various situations you think may arise.

5. Take a supportive and trusted person along with you
Consider rehearsing with them ahead of time.

6. It is OK to avoid places that trouble you
You don't have to ride by the scene of the accident today. You can choose when you want to ride in a car. You can't control everything, but you have a right to a voice. You can be gentle to yourself today and take a challenge tomorrow.

7. Put your needs and feelings first
You don't have to take care of everyone else right now. And if you have to do something, do it on terms that make you most comfortable.

> **8. See your doctor**
> If you feel overwhelmed, your doctor may help with the new anti-anxiety medications.
>
> **9. Find out what works for you**
> Do that — not what anyone else thinks you should do.

Emotional Swings

People often find themselves reacting more intensely to situations than they did before.

"The night after the accident I was in the car with my husband driving. We were at an intersection. He pulled out quickly between two cars. Objectively, it wasn't that it was so bad, but I was real scared. I suddenly felt terrified. I picked up the newspaper I was reading and covered my face.

"My emotions were right on the edge again. At first he couldn't understand. He told me I was overreacting. Later he apologized. I wouldn't have reacted that way before the accident. I know that's how he drives, but now it really gets to me. Later, I felt so down. I couldn't figure out why."

It is not surprising to hear people talk of the roller-coaster ride of abrupt highs and lows after an accident. Everything feels amplified.

It is not uncommon to find your emotional balance upset for a period after the accident.

Crying Spells

Even a truck driver cannot control his spontaneous reactions to a near miss.

"I was driving down the right lane on a four-lane road. A flatbed truck in the left lane was hauling a full load of concrete

storm drainpipe — big, wide pipe 30 feet long. He was going too fast for the road, so I stayed way back.

"When we got some curves, he swerved. The load started to tip, so he jerked the truck back. The top of the truck just caught a bridge abutment. It sheared off the chains holding the pipe and they all rolled onto the road. The guy next to me and I had to dodge through the pipes and the chunks of concrete. We finally got through and I pulled over to the side of the road. As I thought about what might have happened, I just burst into tears. I never cry, but I couldn't help it. I wasn't in control.

"After the accident, I was afraid to ride in a car. I couldn't sleep at night. I'd cry over the littlest thing."

The upset leads some to make tremendous efforts.

Bobbie was upset with herself because she found herself crying whenever she thought about the accident. Then she tried to restrain herself from crying. "I try never to cry now because I feel that if I start I will never be able to stop."

Giddiness

"Whenever my girlfriend (who was in the accident with me) and I get together, we act very giddy and laugh at the silliest things. People will sometimes look at us, and I think, 'Oops.' "

This is not just a female trait. Police officers, fire fighters, EMTs, and undertakers all have their own form of private gallows humor. It is a way of warding off tensions of the job or the accident.

"I try to keep laughing; otherwise, I'd burst into tears."

Emotional Numbness

The antidote to the emotional roller coaster is to shut off the system. You may not be aware of it, but others may comment that you do not seem to react to things the way you did before.

Sometimes people are very aware of it and report that they deliberately shut off feelings just to get through the time.

Paul's van was hit by an airplane. The propeller tore up the van and nearly hit Paul. Paul was shaken up but relieved to be alive. He retold the episode for several days.

Several weeks later a fuel truck ran into his new van at nearly the same spot. Fuel spilled all around him, but fortunately did not ignite. Paul left that job at the airport in two weeks. When asked about the accidents, Paul replied with a straight face that they had not affected him.

Paul quickly became numb to the deadly prospects of his work. More often, in the first weeks, the numbing is more subtle. Listen to Jane, who survived a head-on collision.

"I spent a lot of time in the hospital taking care of everyone else. I was not really allowing myself to feel much pain.

"Barb [Jane's friend who was driving the car that was hit head-on] was wheeled down to see me. She was so pissed. 'That guy ruined my life. I hope he dies.' She was just so angry. I couldn't understand it. I thought she was being overly dramatic. Her injuries were more than mine. I was the lucky one. Everyone kept saying, 'You're so lucky.' I bought that. 'Yeah, it's true,' I said.

"I didn't really let myself get angry. Maybe a little bit. I hadn't eaten the whole time I was in the hospital. People were starting to comment on my weight. I was furious about that. 'Of course I'm thin! I've been in the hospital for a week not eating anything but Jell-O.' "

Jane deliberately blocked out the anger and talked herself out of feelings until she was ready.

"It wasn't for a long time — a year, even two years — that I allowed myself to get angry. But Barb was angry right away.

> **"I spent a lot of time in the hospital taking care of everyone else. I was not really allowing myself to feel much pain."**

'He ruined my life,' she said. 'Come on!' I thought. 'In a few months, we'll be fine.' I didn't say that out loud, but that's what I was thinking to myself. I said to myself, 'Hey! I'm alive.'"

Jane's comments are a valuable illustration of the contradictory impulses of car accident stress. On the one hand she is being oblivious to her own terror and anger. Yet the anger finds expression in more oblique ways.

Isolation and Feeling Alone

"At first, everyone was so concerned and eager to help. Then they wanted me to get on with my life. I didn't feel like anyone really understood what I had been through. I felt so alone."

You are different than you were before the accident. You look at things differently. People who haven't been through the accident are not having the same reactions. They are just like you were before the accident and the way you wish you could be again. They don't understand you, and you may even resent the fact that they don't have to go through what you have to endure.

It is not something that can be easily explained. So you tend to retreat and check people out thoroughly before you trust them. Even then, the slightest misstep can lead you to withdraw, thinking:

Better alone than misunderstood, having to endure the advice of people who haven't a clue about me.

"My Pain"

"No one can understand what I have been through."

When her husband roared in front of the other car, Rachel felt terrified. She cringed as she imagined the crash all over again. She began to explain. Henry gave her a withering look and she gave up. "He'll never understand. He thinks I'm just overreacting," she thought.

People tend to feel psychologically isolated after an accident. Those in the accident feel that anyone who wasn't there can't possibly understand. Those in accidents where there was injury or death feel that people who lost only their cars cannot possibly understand their pain. Women will feel that men can't understand and vice versa.

At first the only connection you may make is with someone you can identify with, someone whose age, sex, and situation are so like yours that it is eerie. Their words seem to have come out of your mouth.

You can begin to appreciate other people's pain again only after you have worked through your own — fully accepting it, making room in your heart for that pain, and becoming willing to go on despite it.

> **You can begin to appreciate other people's pain again only after you have worked through your own — fully accepting it, making room in your heart for that pain, and becoming willing to go on despite it.**

Disorientation

Philip had lunch with me the day after his accident. He asked for my card, and I gave it to him. He put it in his coat pocket. A few minutes later, he asked if I had given him my card. Later, as we were leaving the restaurant, he stopped his car in the driveway, backed up, and went back in to look for his glasses. They were on his nose.

Your mind will be absorbed with tasks related to the accident. You will find yourself absentmindedly getting from one place to another and then suddenly feeling disoriented and wondering how you got there.

Difficulty Concentrating

A college soccer team was riding in a van that was sideswiped at an intersection. The accident happened just before final exams for the semester. In the weeks following the accident, team members found that they would read a chapter in a textbook and by the time they were finished they could not re-member what they had read.

The mind has only a limited capacity for attention. When you are involved in an accident, part of the attention previously devoted to other matters is now taken up with reorganizing your thoughts and sorting through the accident. You don't have room for many other concerns. You may feel you are losing your mind . . . or that something is dreadfully wrong . . . that you will never get back to "normal." It's not true. You will find a new "normal"; you just have other business to attend to right now.

Memory Problems and Feeling Distracted

"It feels weird to me because things seem to distract me so easily from what I am doing. Sometimes I forget where I am, how I got here, or what I was doing a few moments ago. I know I'm not crazy, but sometimes I feel so scattered I begin to wonder."

You may find yourself distracted easily and unable to focus as well as you normally do. This is another by-product of reflection. It demonstrates the ease with which memories, intrusive thoughts, and connections related to the accident come so swiftly to mind. As your mind is figuring out what happened — why it happened and what it all means — you have less capacity to focus on what are, in comparison, trivial things — like eating, sleeping, and paying bills.

You may also begin to think you are going crazy after an accident because your memory is not working as usual. You may be forgetful, misplacing things.

Your mind has limits. When you are absorbed with figuring out if you will live or recover, or if you can trust other drivers, you have less mental energy to devote to smaller, everyday things that you used to be able to remember. Be gentle with yourself. Allow yourself the room to have these reactions. Don't push yourself or leap to conclusions like, "I'll always be like this!" or "It will never get better."

Many indicators of stress reactions and the process outlined above may apply in a slightly different form to you. Therefore, consider how you will attend to your own reactions before you get too concerned about helping your survivor with their problems.

Men and Women

Frequently, there are differences in how men and women show their reactions.

For years, many public safety officers — cops, firefighters, EMTs, emergency room staff, and especially their supervisors — would tell me that they didn't react to the tragic events they constantly dealt with. "You can't let it get to you," they would say. They really meant, "If you don't pay attention, it won't affect you." What finally seemed to have an impact were studies that began to emerge. On average, male police officers and firefighters died at age 57, years before men in other occupations. This figure was derived after deaths due to on-the-job hazards were considered. Now these professionals are beginning to address these stresses. They recognize that even if they don't express their stress-related emotions, the reactions still show themselves in their health, their drinking and eating patterns, and their social lives.

Men are more likely than women to react in this "tough-it-out" fashion. But as women take up those roles, they begin to adopt those same postures. It's useful on the job. You don't want an emergency medical technician at the scene of an accident complaining, "Oh, no! I can't stand the sight of blood." You want them to get you out and to the hospital. Therefore, their damped reactions may be more noticeable to others. Stoic people are more likely to express their reactions in high blood pressure and in their behavior rather than in their "feelings."

The point is that just because one is not aware does not mean the reactions are not there. A cut still bleeds even if numbed with an anesthetic which kills the pain.

Women may be more aware of their reactions but are more likely to worry that they are going "crazy" or that something is really wrong with them. Sensitive people may find themselves labeled by the common misconception that reactions are a sign of weakness.

Of course, these are general observations. Men and women come in all types and sizes, and each man or woman has a unique "package" of reactions.

Stoic people are more likely to express their reactions in high blood pressure and in their behavior rather than in their "feelings."

SUMMARY

Reactions to the accident come in a whole "package." And it is a "package" deal. You can't pick and choose. Your set of reactions will include feelings, memories, bodily reactions, and changes in your behavior. The array of indications laid out here will help you recognize your package. Then you can make it a tool of your recovery. The package is part of your bill. And it remains due, even if you shove it aside.

---

[9] I am indebted to Dr. Les Wyman of the Gestalt Institute of Cleveland for his wonderful conception of the "package" of reactions.
[10] Dawn Gregerson, Volvo ad, 1992.

12

Why Am I Alive?
What Did I Do?
Guilt and Personal Responsibility

Survivor Guilt

If one person in an accident survives, the "What ifs" and "If onlys" frequently take the form of: "Why did I survive?"

Driving her 80-year-old mother home on the rain-slicked freeway, Adele lost control as a passing truck sent a wall of water over her car, and she slid into another trailer truck. She awoke to realize her mother was dead beside her. Later in the hospital, she agonized over why she had survived. For several weeks, she fired psychiatrists and made all the hospital staff dislike her until someone came in and asked why she felt like such an evil person.

Such "survivor" guilt can affect even the grateful parents of a spared child.

Jeremy went off fishing with his teenaged friends. They were headed up a hill behind a truck. Staring into the early morning sun, they failed to see the truck ahead. The car ran into the truck, severing its brake line. The truck halted, then began swiftly slipping backward. The truck ran into the car, killing the boy next to Jeremy. Though he was badly cut and had internal injuries, Jeremy managed to crawl out and dragged one of his friends to safety.

"It was my fault, you know. Daddy asked me which toy store I wanted to go to. If I hadn't said to go to the bigger one, we wouldn't have had the accident."

The boy who died lived down the street. There was an open house for friends and family. Feeling thankful that it was Jeremy who had been spared, Jeremy's father refused to go. His wife was reluctant to go and highlight the father's absence. Fifteen years later, Jeremy's mother still feels pangs of guilt over the episode.

In this case, the father's joy over his son's survival fed guilt over the thought: "Better his son died than mine." Such survival guilt is always amplified when there is some element of action by the individual — Adele was driving the car her mother was killed in — Jeremy's father's "selfish" gratitude kept him from the service for the other family.

What Did I Do? — Personal Responsibility

The "what ifs," "if onlys," and reevaluations are especially harsh and wracking when it comes to you.

Jane had been a passenger in a head-on crash. She was troubled by her thoughts in the days before the accident.

"At the same time, I was thinking about the accident. I was trying to make sense out of it. Why did it happen? A week before the accident, a girlfriend had written me about being in an institution. She wrote flippantly that she had tried suicide. She was bored with her life.

"I wanted to talk with her because I was feeling depressed, too. I hated LA and I wanted out. I knew what I needed to do, but I didn't have the courage to do it. I didn't like myself very much.

"Then the night before the trip, Bruce and I had a fight. He walked out. I was so upset I called a help line for the first time ever. I talked to a stranger. All of this stuff was going through my mind. I actually was thinking about taking my own life.

"For a long, long time after the accident, a year or more, I blamed myself for the accident. I thought I had created the whole thing. Somehow I thought I had the ability to create this accident."

Jane did not choose this agonizing form of reflection. She took on guilt for the accident as her mind wove the events of the previous week and the accident together.

It was up to Jane to unweave it. She could not depend on her husband to help. Bruce had nothing to do with the accident directly. But, while Jane was conflicted over bringing the accident about, Bruce began to reevaluate his imagined behavior and compare his own role to others' . . .

"Afterwards, I went through all this guilt about . . . should I have been braver and just raced across the road? What kind of husband am I? . . . It didn't hit me then, but as I was thinking about it afterwards and during the next few days, I felt I should have rushed right across the street.

"It was something that I thought about a lot, particularly because . . . Lynn's brother, John, was in a car right in front of Lynn and Jane. So he saw the accident take place in the rear view mirror. He stopped his car immediately, jumped out . . . was Johnny on the spot . . . a hero . . . tore off the door of the car, got Jane out of the car, out onto the pavement, and got a blanket wrapped around her.

"You know, he was really a hero. I thought, 'Would I have been able to do that? How would I have reacted? What would I have done?' It bothered me."

Jane, who had been in the passenger seat during the crash, struggled with her own sense of responsibility. On a very different track, Bruce's shocked state at the scene evoked painful and continuing criticism of what he saw as his own failure. It didn't matter that he wasn't there to tear off the door. Logic does not drive this process. Two years later, he was still haunted by his imagined behavior.

Other nonparticipants can sometimes see their behavior more omnipotently.

Danielle, Tom's wife, had been harried taking care of their child alone and seeing her own patients while Tom had been away at the conference. When he got back, Danielle expressed irritation at Tom that she had been stuck with the work while he got a break at the conference. The next morning, Danielle insisted that Tom take their daughter, Natalie, out to buy a gift for a birthday party. As Tom and Natalie walked out the door, Danielle breathed a sigh of relief and whispered under her breath, "Good riddance!"

You may suspect what went through her mind when she got the phone call notifying her of the accident. In the days after the accident, Danielle saw her role and her comment as having caused the tragedy.

"If only I hadn't sent them off in anger. He probably knew it and that is why he was distracted."

This is one striking aspect of listening to people after a tragedy. Invariably, the first person you criticize is yourself.

Even Tom and Danielle's daughter, Natalie, thought she was to blame. In classic fashion, Natalie illustrated how children often use play to act out their reactions.

The day after the accident, Natalie was getting ready for school. She was dressed, and a friend staying to help noticed her playing with her hairbrush. Natalie had put two of her tiny dolls on the brush and was guiding the brush with the dolls on it around the carpet. Asked what she was doing, Natalie replied that she was going to buy the birthday present with Dad. Suddenly she announced, "It was my fault, you know. Daddy asked me which toy store I wanted to go to. If I hadn't said to go to the bigger one, we wouldn't have had the accident."

Here were all three members of the family blaming themselves: Tom, in the hospital, berating himself for not paying attention, Danielle reproaching herself for feeling relieved they were going, and Natalie chiding herself for picking the "wrong" store.

What does it tell us? In crises, human beings will go to great lengths to maintain control, to continue to see themselves as in charge of events. Sometimes the cost of that myth of control is to assume the blame for the accident. Some counselors suggest that one should dismiss the distorted blame. As a therapist, I find this an error. I want to listen, ask questions, invite reflection over time, and try to learn what is at the root of the personal blame. Telling someone it is not their fault may be partially true. But it shortcuts the process of you learning it for yourself. And it also forecloses an important and potentially liberating lesson. By exploring how you did or did not exercise your own power then, you are free to see what you can do in your life now.

Later questioning revealed that Natalie had a hidden agenda. She wanted to go to the second store not just to buy the gift for her friend's party, but because there was a toy there she was hoping she could persuade her father to buy for her. When Natalie was offered the opportunity to talk, she revealed this further source of her distress and was then able to separate the secret motivation to get the toy for herself from any responsibility for the accident. That enabled her to talk more freely about her fears following the accident. She could accept her powerlessness over what she could not control, and she saw that by voicing her concerns to her dad, she could also exercise her personal power.

SUMMARY

The first thing people do in evaluating an accident is to privately review their own behavior. Their sense of guilt and personal responsibility is usually distorted. It needs to be examined further, as it is an important key to recovery.

13

Depression Is Actually Progress

It may seem strange to you, but depression is a hopeful development in the progress through the digestion phase.

Depression

Depression is a common response after you have exhausted all the earlier stages of digestion.

"I'd just feel so down all of a sudden. Nothing seemed to matter much."

This is what all the earlier stages have been in tension over. Now that the earlier forms of denial, bargaining, anger and blame are not as effective, the reality is naked before you. The closer you come to fully absorbing the reality of what the accident has meant, the nearer you skirt to depression. Depression is the signal that reality has sunk in.

"It will never change. I'll never have a real life again."

It is not surprising that you feel down. Important things that you thought and felt have been shaken up. All the things that have changed suddenly can seem so overwhelming and insurmountable. The losses seem so final and so devastating. Your perspective has changed as a result of the accident. Everything that was not right, but tolerable, before the accident can suddenly seem unmanageable. You seem to devalue your assets and focus only on your liabilities.

"It will never change. I'll never have a real life again."

It is a phase, another stage of digestion. And the only way to the other side is through it. While you grapple with this depression, you may still notice other forms of reflection and distraction. That's natural. But now you can use some tools to get over this hurdle.

What to Do — With Depression [11]

Remember that depression is an expected and even hopeful reaction. While you are in it, there are some things you can do. First try the "Things You Can Do Right Now" in Chapter Nineteen. They work for depression as well as other reactions. Make a list of things you are willing to try.

Then select from the following suggestions to add to your list for help with your depression. Of course, if your depression gets out of hand, it's time to let a professional help.

Get up and do something
The urge to crawl into bed and hibernate is typical during depression. Don't give in to it. Do something, anything, with someone you like. Change where you are and who you are with.

Try illumination
Some cases of depression, particularly in women, are related to Seasonal Affective Disorder (SAD). With winter's shorter days and weaker sun providing less light in their lives, some people become deeply depressed. Light therapy, in which they are exposed to bright light for several hours during the day, miraculously brings people out of the doldrums.

Give in

For a day, don't fight the depression and just give in to it. Say to yourself, "OK, I feel like a frog in a bog today, so I'm just going to go to sleep early. When I wake up tomorrow, I'm going to feel much better." Don't, however, give in tomorrow. Get back to this list.

But don't give up

Remember that today you may feel down, but tomorrow is a new day. All these reactions have passed for others . . . and they will pass for you too. Keep in mind that your *attitude* does not have to depend on your *feelings*. You can be *up* even when you are feeling down.

Call for help

If you are too depressed to take any of the other steps, call your spouse, friend, doctor, or counselor as your first line of support. If possible, program your phone with their numbers. Then, in an emergency, all you have to do is push one panic button.

If your depression hangs on stubbornly, consult your doctor, a therapist, or a treatment center. Or call a help line. (Speaking to a trained and sympathetic stranger can be very liberating.) You may need additional outpatient or inpatient treatment or professional help from someone trained in traumatic stress.

If you are willing to work through the depression, it will only be a temporary stage of digestion. Unexpected gifts will appear in your life.

Insight and Silver Lining

Sometimes depression allows us to see the light, to make lemonade out of lemons.

Sometimes the darkness of depression allows us to see the light . . . to make lemonade out of lemons. Your perspective changes.

"But for every bad, there is a good. And in this case, it was goodness of [those people who stopped]. They had stopped, [comforted me], eased me back into my car, put a blanket around me, and called the police. God heard my prayer and sent them to me. I hate that they were needed, but I'm glad they were there."[12]

After you make a new connection you can suddenly see bad things in a different light. A dreary path that seemed endless now has a ray of hope. Insight involves reexamining the pieces in a new light, putting the puzzle together in a new way with a piece you had overlooked. Each insight is a marker on the road to full recovery. They mark the end of the digestion phase.

Acceptance

Listen to how tragedy changed one sheriff's outlook.

Tears welled up in his eyes as he described the destruction... He said the experience had changed how he viewed his job. "My focus used to be, how many people can we arrest and how many can we put away? After twenty years, I'm thinking more, how can I help the community? What can I do?" [13]

This sheriff has accepted the reality. He has struck out on a search for a new "survivor mission" — a new way of doing his job, of living his life, by bearing witness to the values forged from the tragedy.[14]

Acceptance means abandoning cynicism and going forward with peace in your heart.

The third phase of the recovery process comes with this kind of acceptance. Acceptance means taking in — without struggle or complaint — all that has happened. It means gradually adjusting your expectations and assumptions, abandoning cynicism, and then going forward with peace in your heart.

Trish, a survivor of a bad crash, found that a quote from Richard Bach helped her find acceptance:

"There is no such thing as a problem without a gift for you in its hands."[15]

Death at an Early Age

This following story from a column by Anna Quindlen of the *New York Times* is not about a car accident but nicely sums up what acceptance is about.

Today is Thanksgiving, and I won't be writing my column. Norma Perkins-Murray, who runs a home day-care center in Aurora, Illinois, wrote it for me.

Norma and I don't know one another, except as intimate strangers, reader and writer. Today she is the writer. These are excerpts from a letter she wrote to me that began, "I feel as if I know you. . . . When you quit your job to stay home with your daughter, Maria, I coincidentally quit mine to stay home with my newborn daughter, Erin.

"I had been working in the business world for 18 years. I discovered I loved staying home, and my husband and I started a day-care home to stay home with Erin and her older brother, Heath. . . . From the start, Erin was independent. She walked early and talked early but went to bed late.

"In late August we took Erin on her first vacation. We went to the Boundary Waters Canoe Area in Minnesota. We stayed in a wonderful cabin, canoed, fished, and picked blueberries. She had the time of her life so far.

"Then the night before we were to leave, she was throwing rocks in the lake off the dock and apparently fell in and drowned. I was taking a shower at the time, her brother was chopping wood, and her dad was cooking on the grill in plain view of her. When he didn't see her for a while, he assumed she came in the cabin with me, since it was getting dark and a little chilly.

"When I came out of the cabin, we began the frantic search for a little girl who had never been away from her parents ever. They had boats with searchlights and dogs in the woods. Everyone kept saying that they would find her, but I knew better. . . . How could this happen to us? She had her lifejacket on every minute she was in the canoe. We just didn't think of everything.

"She was missed at 7 and they found her at 10, in 7 feet of water, 10 feet off the end of the dock.

"A friend recommended Conley Funeral Home. . . . When we saw Erin for the first time, she was tucked into a bed in a room with a night light. Bruce Conley said we could spend as much time with her as we wanted. We could wash her hair. . . . We could dress her in her special dress. Those were both the hardest and most painful things but the most wonderful, meaningful things I had ever done.

"The next day was the children's program where they explained that Erin's body didn't contain her spirit anymore, much like when a sea creature leaves its shell. Then we went upstairs and let each of the children with their parents see her, touch her, and say goodbye.

"We had buried her in the cemetery where I go jogging

and can see her whenever I go. . . . We let the children throw flowers in and after some singing, set some white balloons with pink ribbons free. We looked up at the balloons going up toward the perfectly blue sky with their pink tails spinning, and my nephew said, 'They look like sperm.' And he was right! The minister said, 'Well, it is the beginning of life.'

"How are we doing? After two months of being ripped apart by conflicting emotions, of reading everything written on near-death experiences, reincarnation, angels, and life after death, I have decided that Erin existed here to change us for the better. . . . I feel her presence around me occasionally and sometimes see her in dreams.

"Why am I telling you all this? Compared to some of the horrible things going on in the world today, it's not the worst thing that could have happened. . . . I know that our funeral service was not typical. Maybe I want you to tell parents that something like this exists, so that they can make a choice. It certainly helped me.

"But maybe I want to point out how our culture avoids talking about death and dying and makes it some sort of medical failure, something to be evaded at all costs, when it could be a time of great healing and comfort.

"Perhaps I want to appreciate the fact that your daughter is alive, or want everyone to know about little Erin Rose Murray and her short, wonderful life."

Done, Norma. I will count my blessings today. And the rest of you count yours.[16]

You have come far along the path of your journey. Congratulations! Part of your mission now will be to pass that peace you have gained on to others.

This has been an abbreviated discussion of insight and acceptance. The second volume in this set, on later reactions, deals more with the obstacles and steps to insight and acceptance.

SUMMARY

Depression is actually an important step forward. It means the reality of the accident has settled in. Depression sets the stage for acceptance — making lemonade of the lemons.

[11] These recommendations are adapted from *The Recovery Book* (1993) by Al Mooney, M.D., Arlene Eisenberg, and Howard Eisenberg, published by Workman Publishing, New York.

[12] Carter, Shelley. "Rain, terror and a drunk driver on a dark road." *Cleveland Plain Dealer*, November 26, 1991, p. C1.

[13] Stewart, James B. "Battle on the Sny." *New Yorker*, August 9, 1993, p. 39.

[14] Robert Jay Lifton first traced this "survivor mission" in the survivors of Hiroshima. From Lifton, Robert Jay (1967), *Death in Life*. New York, Random House, pp. 302-305.

[15] Bach, Richard. (1989) *Illusions: The Adventures of a Reluctant Messiah*. New York, Dell.

[16] Quindlen, Anna. "Public and Private." Op Ed page. *New York Times*, November 25, 1993.

PART THREE:
OTHER ASPECTS

The Dumb Things People Say

People often don't know how to react to other people in pain. In their distress, they say things that end up sounding dumb to you. But those are really ways of dealing with their own discomfort at not knowing what to say.

"It's God's will."

"He only gives you what you can handle."

"They said, 'He only gives these things to people He loves.' I thought, 'If He loves me any more, it's going to be fatal.' "

"People are uncomfortable because they're feeling glad it's not happening to them."

This feeling of relief that the tragedy has not happened to them breeds guilt and confusion. Most people are shocked to find these feelings welling up in them. They are embarrassed that they are relieved and happy it's happening to someone else and not to them. However, these feelings are natural, and it's our ability to accept these feelings of relief and still not flee that makes us a truly compassionate friend.

Some people may turn inquisitor and quickly pass judgment on your behavior.

Remember Donna's story of being hit by the elk and driving home through the hail of shattered glass (page 66)?

Donna told her story a few weeks later over dinner to a

> **"They said, 'He only gives these things to people He loves.' I thought, 'If He loves me any more, it's going to be fatal.' "**

> **"People are uncomfortable because they're feeling glad it's not happening to them."**

group of friends. One very close friend vehemently challenged her. "You didn't say anything about what you felt. Tell us! Why didn't you go back for the elk? Why did you drive all that way? Why are you telling us this story?"

As other friends questioned the vehemence of her response, Donna's friend revealed a previous accident she had had and acknowledged that Donna's tale had aroused several unresolved reactions about her own accident in her.

A woman who lost her husband was very perceptive about how people reacted to her.

"Not knowing what to say makes people uncomfortable so they try to get my mind off my problems. They invite me places. They feel they need to cheer me up.

"They say, 'It's not good for you to be sitting around the house this way.'"

Or others will try to shift to a positive focus.

"'You should be thankful for the 12 good years you had together.' It's not that I didn't treasure our 12 years together, but that didn't lessen my sense of loss right then."

"They told me, 'In a few years, this will be just a bad dream. You're young. You'll get over it.'"

Even the financial settlement is supposed to cover the loss.

"With that settlement, you've got it made!"

Sometimes people project their dissatisfactions with their own lives, their own jobs, their own marriages onto you.

Sometimes people project their dissatisfactions with their own lives, their own jobs, their own marriages onto you.

"How lucky you are that your mother is dead," someone told Adele. "You won't have to go through all that grief in a nursing home with her."

"Why couldn't it have been the SOB I'm married to? Your

husband was so nice. If my husband was dead, I'd have no problems."

Sometimes it seems the only thing you can do is ignore them or withdraw.

"Nobody wants to understand."

Ours is a practical society. We are trained to insulate ourselves from many of life's difficulties. Most of us no longer are familiar with or have much experience in how to cope with tragedy and sudden death. And those people who do acknowledge pain and hurt in themselves are often belittled for a lack of "toughness." Ironically, that "toughness" is a shield to mask very deep hurt. Such "tough it out" people have difficulty with their own pain and, therefore, with yours. Don't let their attitude deter you from your recovery. They may have deferred looking at their bill, but you can make your own choice. And the wisdom of others who have recovered is here to help you.

Family, Friends, and Neighbors

Sometimes you end up being the one doing the comforting.

"I ended up trying to console other people. I'm the one telling them it's OK."

"I had two friends come to the hospital. They were crying their eyes out. I said, 'There, there.' I thought, I'm the one injured, but I'm taking care of them."

People who see you every day, who love you, sometimes see the implications of your injuries before you do. They see immediately how much worse it could have been. They figure out the dimensions of the loss more quickly, and even, at first, may feel them more keenly. Then, you find yourself in the role of the comforter, helping them through your tragedy.

As the weeks pass, most of your friends and neighbors will get impatient. Remember Clive and Ann from the Stress Bill

> "Tough it out " people have difficulty with their own pain and, therefore, with yours.

> "I had two friends come to the hospital. They were crying their eyes out. I said, 'There, there.' I thought, I'm the one injured, but I'm taking care of them."

"Friends become uncomfortable with you after a while. They don't want to hear."

chapter — how Ann wanted Clive to focus on the wedding, not on his missing teeth? Family, friends, and neighbors want to focus on the future and go on with their own lives. They assume you are able — or should be able — to do the same. They expect you to control your pain, your fears, your grief, your tears . . . and to be strong.

"Friends become uncomfortable with you after a while. They don't want to hear."

"People just couldn't understand. They were going home to their families, their problems."

"You just don't realize 'till it happens to you."

Luckily, there are some people who do understand, who instinctively, or through their own experiences, know the right thing to do.

"One friend just let me talk. She didn't say a word. She just listened. She was great. She didn't try to tell me what to do."

It is very important to find someone who will let you talk, who will listen without judging what you say. Sometimes the people best able to understand are those who have been through a tragedy themselves — other survivors. They can understand your pain and will share their own experiences, explaining how they handled situations without feeling compelled to advise you on the only way to do things.

God, the Church, the Mosque, and the Temple

Family and friends are not the only ones who can seem to say the wrong thing. Claire reacted to a priest who told her he understood how she felt when her husband was killed.

"I went into church ready to do battle. How dare that priest tell me what it's like. He's never even had kids!"

Sometimes we are disappointed when people we look up to don't know what to say.

"I wanted answers. Of course, I never got any."

Our reactions to God, the church, the mosque, and the temple are expressions of our different styles of reactions. The accident draws on different parts of you. For some, beliefs have been a real help and strength.

"I felt that a Great Someone had been watching over me every step of the way."

"If it hadn't been for the church, I'd never have made it."

For others, it now is a time when doubts become amplified.

"What kind of a God would let this happen?"

Anger at the pastor, the rabbi, the imam, and God are very common. Yet, even in rejection, you often reassert spiritual values.

Sharon lost her firefighter husband in a crash. Though she found herself alienated from God, spiritual values came through in her response to their children.

"I'm their mother. I have certain responsibilities to see them through this. I found myself focusing on the values that Dad stood for: courage, devotion to service, facing tough situations and seeing them through even at danger to himself . . . values I want for the children."

This process of examining, rejecting, and often reaffirming, in new ways, shared values with your family is an essential part of recovery. Both reliance and rejection can be strong indicators of a natural reaction to tragedy. You can go through periods feeling a great need for the strength and love that God and the church, mosque, or temple can give you. At other times, you

Anger at the pastor, the rabbi, the imam, and God are very common. Yet, even in rejection, you often reassert spiritual values.

may experience feelings of great bitterness and anger toward God for allowing such a tragedy to happen.

"It took me a long time to get over my anger. But now I have made my peace with God, and I am very comfortable at services again."

SUMMARY

You expect that what other people say will be helpful. However, people often say silly things. It stems from their powerful reactions to the accident. And then you sometimes comfort them. Even your spiritual leaders may not know what to say. Your responses to God and religion may be tested by the accident.

CHAPTER

15

What to Say and Do
When You Don't Know
What to Say or Do

Let's look first at the best kinds of things to say. The best things that we can say to accident survivors are things that are truthful and helpful. It is a form of "emotional first aid" [16] that you can provide through these simple statements:

"I'm sorry it happened."

"I'm glad you're as OK as you are."

"I'm willing to just be there with you or to just listen when you want to talk. You be in charge."

The truth, however painful it may seem to you, is always best. Sugar coating your words does not help the survivor.

What Not to Say and Do [17]

Now let's look at some of the things that sound dumb to survivors (and may interfere with their recovery). Some things you want to say or do stem from an impulse to fix it or make it better for the survivor. The following are things people want to do or say that don't work well.

"I'm willing to just be there with you or to just listen when you want to talk. You be in charge."

Avoid

Telling survivors that everything is or will be all right. It doesn't feel all right now. And you don't really know what it will be like!

Avoid

Telling survivors that you know how they feel. No matter how much you think you know about what people go through, you don't know exactly how this person feels. Let him or her tell you and just listen.

Avoid

Trying to force survivors to talk about any details of the accident which they are reluctant to tell. Let them set the pace, decide when they are ready, and choose the person they want to talk to.

Avoid

Judging the conduct or feelings of the survivors. Just listen . . . That's the hardest thing to do!

Avoid

Asking questions that implicitly blame the survivor for the accident. "Why were you driving so fast?" implies your "if only." Instead, listen to the questions they ask themselves.

Avoid

Telling the survivor "It's not your fault." Depriving them of their questions about their own actions turns them into victims and robs them of their integrity. Be willing to listen, to hear their judgments of themselves and others. Their judgment may be far more severe than your own. By listening, you can help the survivor give voice to the unmentionable. Only after confronting the judgment can they arrive at their own more balanced perspective, recapture their integrity, and plot their course so "it" won't happen again.

Avoid

Ignoring the needs of other co-survivors, the family, and the concerned others who are also affected.

Avoid

Letting yourself remain impatient with an upset survivor. You may feel impatient, but that is your feeling to confront. It is normal for most survivors to have reactions and to take days, weeks, months, and even years to recover from the experience. And they must set the pace, not conform to your timetable.

You have to listen to yourself before you can truly listen to the survivor.

What to Say and Why It Works[18]

Now let's look at the reasons why some things work better than others.

Do

Pay attention to your own reactions. The concerned other often cannot deal with the pain and the tears of the survivor. In your mind, you stand in the survivor's place and imagine what it must be like and how much it must hurt. Doing this is natural. But such thoughts have to do with your vulnerability, not the survivor's. You have to listen to yourself before you can truly listen to the survivor.

Do

Let the survivor choose. If the survivor can't find a way to talk, it just delays the process. Talking moves the survivor toward acceptance. For a variety of reasons, they may not be able to talk to you right now. Maybe you are too close for comfort. Perhaps you remind them of something they can't face yet. Let them choose the time, the place, and the person to talk with. Do not take the survivor's unwillingness to talk with you personally. They will find the time to talk to you.

Do

Listen first. When the time comes, your task is to listen first, not to talk. Let the survivor know what you have heard from what they have said — not your analysis of it, or what they should have said, but their ideas, in their words. Remember that you don't have to do, correct, or fix anything.

The need to fix it is what immobilizes you. As a concerned person, you think that if the one you love is feeling something deeply, you somehow have to ease the pain, make it better. You don't. Listening and understanding is a great gift. You are allies to the survivors, accepting the choices and detours they make, knowing that the survivors carry within the tools and the strength to heal.

Your best help comes from the posture of ally, not caretaker.

"I know you can do it, handle it, and get through it. I am here to help and be there with you. Do it in your own time and in your own way. I'll be there."

> **Do**
>
> Hesitate and reflect before speaking. There is great power and beauty in silence. Let the survivor feel what they are feeling. Just be there. As thoughts and reactions arise in you, hesitate and reflect before speaking. Where is this coming from? Generally, it is far better to refrain from offering advice. If your own experience gives you insight, share the source of your learning and strength rather than advice.

The foolish things we say come from our own needs, not the survivor's needs.

Often, over 20 years, as I have listened to survivors, I can feel a thought rising in me. I think I know exactly what they "should" do. When I reflect for a moment, I realize how painful these revelations are for me to hear and how much I want the survivor to stop. If I listen to myself, I find that some experience I've had is being tapped. This is a touchy moment. Most often, I realize it is more relevant to me than the survivor. Then I note it and find my own time and place to reflect on it.

More rarely, by disclosing my own triggered experience, I feel I can illuminate an immediate dilemma the survivor has revealed. Then, I may choose to share it. But rather than giving advice, I share my experience. I don't offer "the" solution. Instead I consider when might be a good moment to share the pain I felt, how it affected me, and what I did. I let the survivor choose any lesson from it.

The foolish things we say come from our own needs, not the survivor's needs.

Don't expect the survivors to be rational or consistent. Stress reactions have their own natural language. It is the language of the heart, not of the head.

Don't try to take away the survivor's fear, pain, or grief. These reactions are part of the healing process. The only way to the other side is through the fear, pain, and grief. Painful as it seems, these reactions speed recovery. Stifling them only delays healing.

Taking time out from listening is OK. If you have been listening for a while and have other things to do, explain that and go do your errands. Survivors may not be able to stop talking when you must stop listening, but that's OK. They are OK, even when they are in pain. That is where, as an ally, you trust in their inner strength. And know that Someone is watching over them.

When you see signs that the survivor is exhausted, drained, and in need of a break, share your observation.

"I see that your eyes have big circles, your body is sagging, and you haven't eaten yet today. Why don't we take a break and make some lunch. Will you help me?"

You benefit from this kind of support, too. You learn from others about grief and tragedy and how to handle them. You receive the gift of being in touch with pain in your own life and seeing how it enriches you.

SUMMARY

Saying the "right thing" doesn't come naturally. Most often there is no "right thing." There are guidelines to what is useful to say and what to avoid. There are keys to listening well and to understanding the role of silence. The major principle is a shift in attitude from caretaker to ally.

[16] I am indebted to NOVA, the National Organization of Victims' Assistance Program of Washington, D.C., for the notion of "emotional first aid" and the substance of the recommendations in their wonderful brochures on Victims of Crime for the core of several of these suggestions. While I differ about the approach to several issues, their distillation in their brochures of the work of many therapists and advocates has been very helpful.

[17] Adapted from the recommendations of NOVA, The National Organization of Victims' Assistance.

[18] Nova, as above.

CHAPTER

16

The Near Miss and
the Fender Bender

"We hit a patch of ice and spun out, and my door flew open. The next thing I knew, I was in a snow bank. I don't remember everything that happened. But fortunately, I was relaxed and landed in the snow. Suddenly, I saw the oncoming cars and realized they were about to skid also. I got up and ran across the highway to get out of the way. There was no damage to the car. And I was fine . . . that day. But the next day I felt like I had been through the clothes dryer for a cycle or two."

You may well be thinking:

"This book doesn't apply to me. Even that was more serious than my accident. Mine was just a near miss or a minor fender bender. No sweat, I've got it covered."

Just as the physical strain above did not show up until the next day, the stress reaction may not be immediately apparent.

Philip went to a cocktail party the night after he was sideswiped and flipped around. People (including his wife) were amazed that he had so little reaction. What they missed was the intense concern Philip now focused on the repair of this favorite car. All his stress reactions were now channeled through the car itself and how well it was cared for.

Remember the adrenaline rush after your near miss? How

No one is saying you were traumatized. Just that you were affected and that you may want to pause for a few minutes and reflect on what it meant to you.

your body trembled when you realized how close you came and how bad it nearly was? Remember when you had to pull over and found yourself shaking afterward? That was an indication that it did affect you. No one is saying you were traumatized. Just that you were affected and that you may want to pause for a few minutes and reflect on what it meant to you.

Listen for a moment to how the sequence played out for Jim and Abby in a recent unreported fender bender.

Jim and Abby were on the way home from a Friday night movie. A Jeep in the right lane suddenly started to make a U-turn. Just as quickly, the driver realized there was oncoming traffic and stopped right in front of Jim.

"Damn!" Jim thought, "I'll never stop this car in time."

Jim jammed on the brakes. Though he was only going 20 mph, the wheels squealed. The Jeep driver finally noticed them . . . and froze. With a car on their right, Jim had nowhere to go. Visions of a terrible crash flickered in the minds of both Abby and Jim as their car continued sliding toward the Jeep. What seemed like an eternity actually took less than two seconds . . . Bam!

Fortunately, the Jeep was canted at an angle, and Jim's bumper hit the rear wheel. Other than a piece of sprung chrome, there was little damage to either car. "Why insist on a fuss?" thought Jim. "It's not much. Let's go," said Abby. Though neither was happy, the formalities were over quickly.

On the way home, Jim's neck began to ache. He had stiffened his legs as he jammed the brake. His arms had been braced against the steering wheel.

"Oh, God! I have no medical insurance," suddenly ran through his head. Abby and Jim had just seen Robert Altman's new film, "Short Cuts," where one character hits a young boy. The boy gets up, insists he is OK, walks home, passes out, and later dies.

Jim and Abby were soon home, arguing over how the driver could have been so stupid, what almost happened, and how it should have been handled.

"You never know what could come up later," Jim remarked, thinking of his neck and possible damage to the Jeep's rear axle. "What if those kids turn up injured? We agreed to walk away."

"It was their fault," Abby insisted.

"As if that ever stopped a lawsuit," countered Jim.

A few minutes later, Jim mentioned that his neck hurt.

Abby snapped, "Whiplash, huh. I was there, too, and I don't have any aches. You're overreacting again."

"My legs and arms were braced trying to stop the damn car," Jim shouted.

Jim felt abandoned by her reaction — shut out. He got angry. "I don't want to talk any more." They went silently to bed.

Jim lay there thinking, "Here we are. Abby's minimizing; I'm blaming. Great argument to have. Abby's numb. Shock really does happen. The accident has affected the trust in our relationship. We are each playing out our fears and arguing over how it was handled."

The next morning Jim and Abby talked again. Jim felt better. Abby casually mentioned a spin-out accident on an icy New York expressway years ago. Jim and Abby retraced their terror and fears of the previous night as they played out several "what ifs" and "if onlys" together. They laughed at how they had displaced their anger at the driver of the Jeep onto each other.

Finally they laid the incident to rest. No claims were filed. The following day, it was as if it had never happened.

As in the case of Jim and Abby, the fender bender generates

its own mini-version of the stress process. But instead of a few days, it's over in a few hours.

Were you stunned that your fender bender happened? Were you relieved that it wasn't worse? Did you find your mind working over the "what ifs" and the "if onlys"? Did you make harsh judgments about the other driver — "Why wasn't he looking out? How could she have done that? Didn't he know what might happen?" Your questions were legitimate, but were they also, like Jim and Abby's arguments, covering up your own fear and relief?

Both the near miss and the fender bender provide an opportunity to reflect. Take a half hour. Allow yourself some quiet time and let what surfaces, surface. Don't judge or manipulate it. Just be there quietly with your reactions. Perhaps some ideas surface about how you are spending your time . . . about why you feel so rushed. Is it time to make some changes in your life? What if the accident had been really bad? What would have happened . . . to your business, your family, you? What is really important? Are you making what's important central in your life? What can you do differently . . . just for today?

Rate your car accident Stress Bill and see how this one stacks up. If you have had previous accidents, are they resolved? Or did some unfinished business surface?

If the accident was minor, you may not have had a full-blown stress reaction. But perhaps a quick glance at the earlier chapters is warranted. Check them out. You will probably realize that, in just the few hours since the accident, you have gone through a mini-version of the recovery process described in this book. It is over for you. Great! Now you can move on with confidence. And pass on this book to someone who needs it.

Near misses and fender benders also generate reactions. However, these reactions are likely to be an abbreviated version of the stress process. Find out how to do a quick check-up. Learn what you can from the accident and move on.

CHAPTER

17

If It Was Very Serious

Handling the Injuries

Jane was hit head-on by a drunk driver. She was in a utility vehicle that saved her life. Let's follow Jane through a few steps in her physical and psychological recovery.

In the Emergency Room

"I was in shock, groggy really. I was starting to feel sore in my chest, my ribs, my back, my legs, even my fingers and feet. I was glad to be alive but not really thinking about anything. 'Here I am. I'm alive. This is weird.'"

The shock cushioned Jane to all that went on and even to her injuries.

"They took me to a hospital and gave me a shot of pain-killer. Again I was saying, 'I'm just fine.' Right before I went under I thought I would die. It was like a weird dream. 'This is death here,' I thought."

Jane's attention was only on whether she was dead or alive and even that was not clear to her.

"The next morning, they woke me up and told me what my injuries were — a cracked pelvis and three broken ribs. I had hit my head on the windshield, and now my eyes were starting to blacken. My whole body was just sore."

> Vanity was gone. Jane didn't care about what she looked like . . . just that she was alive and hurting. And she wanted to be cared for.

Vanity was gone. Jane didn't care about what she looked like . . . just that she was alive and hurting. And she wanted to be cared for.

"The doctor came in every morning at 7:00 a.m. He never touched me, never asked me how I was. He just came in, did his rounds and left. I hated this man. I felt he was not caring. And I wanted care."

She may not have gotten angry with the guy who hit her... but other people did not escape. Her irritation at the doctor was legitimate but was also amplified by the fact that she was not allowing her anger at the driver to surface. So it found other avenues of expression.

"I didn't really let myself get angry. Maybe a little bit. I hadn't eaten the whole time I was in the hospital. People were starting to comment on my weight. I was furious about that. 'Of course I'm thin! I've been in the hospital for a week not eating anything but Jell-O.'"

Others took their frustration out on Jane.

"I was trying to be the best patient. There was a woman across the hall who was just screaming around the clock. She took up all the nurses' time. One morning I woke up about 4 a.m. I couldn't sleep and I was in a lot of pain. So I called for a nurse. She came in and yelled at me, 'What do you want? Can't you see we're busy?'"

Despite the aggravations, Jane appreciated being in the hospital for a while.

"I liked being in the hospital. I liked being taken care of. I could rest."

Going Home

All the fears that were held at bay in the relative safety of the hospital come pouring out as you get back into a car.

"Then we went home. The trip home was really hard. Getting in a car was really, really difficult. It was painful just trying to fit in. Then as we drove, it was frightening. Cars would come up next to us on the freeway and I would just freak."

Recuperating

Adjustments to the accident and its emotional consequences are often postponed until the adjustments to the new physical realities have been managed.

"So we got home, and I was bedridden. I couldn't walk and had to be carried to the bathroom. I was an invalid. I hated that. For the first time in my life, I couldn't hop up and run across the room. I couldn't do things for myself. I was beginning to realize what this meant. My life wasn't my own. I was dependent on someone else. I was frustrated."

Relief that you are alive brings its own set of adjustments for others, too.

"My mother came and stayed with me. For her, I think it was a way to feel in control. Her daughter had been in this accident, had almost lost her life. She had no control over that. She needed to be there . . . to get things back in order . . . for herself."

Conflict develops over the needs of the caretaker and the survivor.

"It was hard because she needed to do for me and I needed to feel like I wasn't completely incapacitated. And at the same time, I wasn't eating and I needed someone to take care of the practical things."

If there have been injuries, that occupies a great deal of your time. Then, what you are facing begins to dawn on you. You may have to adjust to a prolonged recovery time, the loss of a limb, or restrictions that you didn't have before. That requires

> **"The trip home was really hard . . . Cars would come up next to us on the freeway and I would just freak."**

an active adjustment and plenty of quiet conversation with yourself. You will find that you go through all the stages of reaction that Elisabeth Kübler-Ross outlines in her book, *On Death and Dying*. Whether or not you face a death, the loss generates a period of bereavement and adjustment.

FOR THE CONCERNED OTHER

When Someone Was Killed

Sometimes it is even more serious and you, the family, are now the survivors. There are several things you have to face now.

Hearing the News

Don got the dreaded phone call. "I knew immediately what it was when they asked me to come to the hospital, and they didn't reassure me that my wife was OK. Driving down, I was numb but kept running in my mind the fact that she was dead. One of my friends came with me.

"They took me in to identify the body. I saw her lying on that slab. I asked for a few moments alone. She looked so peaceful there. I cradled her broken body in my arms and took some time to say good-bye. I told her all the things I wanted her to part with."

Sometimes the responses of other people are overwhelming, and you have to delay your responses to take care of them as they react to the news.

"My [older] brother, Jon, age 16, departed for a fishing trip in Canada at 5:00 a.m. I awakened, and we talked as he dressed. My last words to Jon that morning were, 'Drive carefully.'

"Returning to our house that night, I heard moaning coming from the kitchen, which I entered cautiously. What I found is indelibly etched in my memory.

"Mom and Dad were on the floor, writhing in excruciating

> "My mother needed to be there . . . to get things back in order . . . for herself."

pain. Dad looked up at me and forced three words out almost soundlessly. The words felt too loud to comprehend.

"Dad said, 'Jon is dead.'

"He had been killed after driving needlessly for twelve hours, crossing the center line, and being struck by an oncoming truck."[19]

At several points we have talked about how the survivors actually end up taking care of others in the first few days. It is both a burden and a relief. Having something to do helps you get through. It allows you to postpone, for a bit, the grief you have.

If You Did It

Sometimes the death you have to face is one that you had a role in.

Lisa had just come home from a year working in London. The next day she was out driving for the first time. A young man on a motorcycle pulled out of a side street right in front of her. She had nowhere to go. She jammed on the brakes, but her car hit him. He had no helmet, and the next day he died of head injuries. Lisa had a terrible time with the nightmares, the "what ifs" and "if onlys."

These are the situations that greatly complicate the recovery process. That is why the book devotes a chapter to personal responsibility.

The Funeral

Don's wife was buried in her hometown. They had a wake in their city and then in her hometown. Don went to the first wake but avoided the second. He had to steel himself for the funeral. "I was afraid of losing it in front of everyone."

Another woman, who lost her husband, took care of everyone else except herself before the funeral.

"It was closed casket because of how he died. Under all the strain, I fainted at the funeral."

The funeral can be a time of great stress. You have been through a great deal by the time it comes. In that impact period, you — and those closest to you — are still digesting it, needing to talk with each other. You don't have to cope alone. You can use family or friends to lean on, to help with decisions. Yet, even in your numbness and your grief, your strength shows through.

"My older brother, Pat, went with me to pick out the casket. He was amazed to see how well his baby sister was handling it."

It can be a time of family solidarity, of protection, of closing of ranks. But the stress can also lead to conflict and discord.

"The in-laws took over. They didn't ask me how I felt. He was their oldest and only son. He and I had talked about the possibility of his death on the job. He had wanted to be buried in his favorite suit and tie. His family arranged with their funeral home to have him buried in his old Army uniform."

Tensions that were there before may now be exaggerated. You have the right to insist that first things come first . . . and that what can be decided or resolved later be put off for now.

The Media

The funeral is also a time when you can no longer keep your grief from becoming public.

"I had refused to see the media, but they came to the funeral with their cameras. I couldn't believe how angry I was at them. I felt invaded and badgered."

Sometimes the tragedy is not yours alone. If your loved ones were public figures, and if the accident was widely reported, your loss becomes a community tragedy. You are asked to bear a greater burden of public grief.

Tensions that were there before may now be exaggerated.

If a teenaged child was injured or killed, everyone with a teenager will identify with your situation and be anxious to hear every bit of information they can. The public grieves through you; therefore, they give you no privacy. The news media are everywhere, and their demand for you is not easily satisfied.

"By the time of the funeral, you resent the notoriety, the publicity."

"The news media... I didn't want any part of it."

"They were camped out front, banging on the door, wanting pictures of us crying, asking terribly prying questions. Someone kept shoving a microphone in my face. They wanted to put us on TV for everybody to see the grieving family."

The pressures of television for images — the competition among TV stations — and the hunger of the public for video to help them with their reactions all drive the media. They can't and won't watch out for you. You have to set the limits and make the decisions. You have that right. It is your choice. You can choose what and how much you want to share with the public.

"I refused to talk to them. If it had been for some good cause to help someone, I would have talked. But all they wanted to do was to catch us at our weakest moments."

"They twisted around what I said. When I told them I didn't know if or when I would go back to work, they said I would quit my job. It caused trouble for me at work."

You do not have to rely on their assurances. Look the media in the eye. Agree on what you will talk about and under what circumstances.

You may be willing to share some things to help others, such as having pictures taken of you and your children. However, you have the right to set your own terms, so that you re-

> **"They were camped out front, banging on the door, wanting pictures of us crying, asking terribly prying questions. Someone kept shoving a microphone in my face."**

tain some control. The media get what they want, but you structure the event so it's safer for you.

"They asked me how I felt . . . I didn't think that people really cared how I felt. I told them that nobody would care tomorrow . . . that by Monday everybody would have forgotten.

"Finally, I said, 'OK, an interview, but no pictures.' They got part of what they wanted and left. They never came back."

Use a trusted friend as a buffer to talk to the media. You make the final decisions but let them protect you.

However you choose to handle it, remember that you do have rights . . . and a choice.

Grief

Coming to terms with the grief of the loss takes time. You can't rush it and "get it over with." Nor can you just ignore it and "make it go away." The process of reflection and distraction described in the earlier chapters of the book applies to this period most forcefully. Pacing yourself through this period is most important. Only partially can you do it on your terms.

Karen took care of everyone else for six months. She had two kids to get through the loss of their father. Her 13-year-old son began to have troubles in school, and she took him to a therapist. Then, one morning, she woke up and realized that there was no one left to take care of except her. When she started to allow her own feelings to surface, she felt overwhelmed. Now there were no distractions, and she was in great pain. She quickly sought help and got just what she needed.

```
┌─────────────────────────────────────────────────┐
│  ▌What to Do — About Grief                       │
├─────────────────────────────────────────────────┤
│                                                  │
│  Grief has its own timing. Memories and recollec- │
│  tions trigger it. If a child died, you will see a │
│  graduation announcement and suddenly become     │
│  aware that you will never celebrate that event.  │
│  When you are thrown into a tragedy, let yourself │
│  feel the pain. If you refuse to allow the grief, │
│  you just build up what you have to do later.    │
│  Though it is exhausting, grieving brings blessed │
│  relief.                                          │
│                                                  │
│  Don't deny your grief. It builds like plaque on  │
│  your emotional arteries and constricts everything│
│  else in your life. Let it flow . . . and feel the│
│  loss and the relief.                             │
│                                                  │
│  There are wonderful texts on bereavement in the  │
│  bibliography at the end of this book. The second │
│  volume of this set deals further with managing   │
│  the grief.                                       │
│                                                  │
└─────────────────────────────────────────────────┘
```

SUMMARY

If the accident was very serious, there are special considerations. Coping with the injuries involves both psychological and physical adjustment. The funeral is a real hurdle. And media attention requires special handling to protect you and your family.

[19] Peter B. Lewis, CEO, in the 1989 Progressive Corporation Annual Report, pp. 4-5, reflecting on the death of his brother, Jon, August 4, 1952.

CHAPTER

18

Dealing with the Kids

The Kids' Reactions

Kids go through their own version of the stress process. At various ages, they express their reactions differently and the effect on them changes. The recommended readings at the end have several excellent references to detailed accounts.

When you are having reactions yourself, it is harder to allow them in your kids. You may find yourself trying to ignore or suppress their reactions, or irritated at how they are handling those reactions. The reactions that irritate you will be the same reactions that you find difficult to accept in yourself.

The first step in helping your kids is to recognize your own reactions. Then you can help them deal with their reactions.

Consider the responses of this family who had a fire in their car.

The car caught fire in the garage after the Bakers returned from a dinner out. The car and the house burned completely. Both the parents and the children, ages 14 and 11, escaped without injury. For months after the fire, the son, who was 14, had insomnia. Finally, he was sent to a therapist who had worked with the family before. What emerged in the session with the therapist was that as the fire was being fought, the boy overheard the fire chief say to a captain, "Five more minutes and they all would have died."

The therapist asked if the boy had appointed himself night

> The kids are a barometer of what is going on in the family. If the adults are trying to bury the impact, then the kids will become the "foghorn," sounding the alarm for the family.

watchman. "Yes," he replied, "I stand guard at night in case the car catches fire again in the garage." The insomnia was not pathological; it was adaptive. The boy was protecting his family. In a family session, when the rest of the family learned what was going on, they agreed first to install smoke alarms, then to share the duty of watching over the car and the house. The boy started sleeping again.

The family had never talked together about the car fire. They had never shared the facts as each of them knew them or their reactions. In "protecting" each other, they were holding off their own recovery.

The Family Debriefing [20]

Brad and Judith had recently been married. They had just come in at the airport with Judith's young son and daughter. As Brad and his stepson, age 8, were loading the luggage in the trunk, an elderly man pulled up behind them. The man was unable to fully stop the car in time. Brad madly waved at him to stop. But the other car's bumper began crushing Brad and Stephen against their car.

Judith saw what was happening. She panicked and began screaming at Brad for allowing her son to be placed in danger. Brad was stunned. Fortunately, Brad's size and the thickness of his legs meant he took all the force. Stephen was protected from injury but badly frightened.

The first step in helping your kids is to recognize your own reactions. Then you can help them deal with their reactions.

That evening, Brad and Judith talked about what had happened. They discussed Judith's panic and screaming at Brad. When they had cleared the air between them, they decided to talk to the kids. Brad and Judith knew they were upset themselves. The kids were upset. They decided to have a family meeting. They gathered the kids with them on the bed and talked through all that had happened. Then they thanked God they were all safe, even if Brad was sore and bruised.

▼ CAR ACCIDENT: A PRACTICAL RECOVERY MANUAL

Brad and Judith had conducted a family debriefing.

In many traumatic situations that affect a family, the family takes care of the physical needs but may neglect the psychological healing that is needed. A family meeting or debriefing can hasten recovery for the whole family.

The kids are a barometer of what is going on in the family. If the adults are trying to bury the impact, then the kids will display the unexpressed distress. They will become the "foghorn," sounding the alarm for the family.

Tragic events can spur greater family harmony and intimacy, if you regard the crisis as an opportunity to bring you closer together.

> **Tragic events can spur greater family harmony and intimacy, if you regard the crisis as an opportunity to bring you closer together.**

Mini-Guide — Organizing the Family Debriefing

Plan the debriefing. Talk together as parents about what you observe and what you want to accomplish. Sort out any tensions between you. Read this mini-guide together first, so you understand the process. Also read the chapters (Chapters Nine through Thirteen) on all the signs of stress reactions. Then you can identify them as they come up and treat them as natural reactions. Make the exercise your own by deciding how you want to organize the debriefing for your family. You don't have to follow a recipe. It's just a guide.

Decide who is going to run the debriefing. It is best if the primary leader is someone who was not as powerfully affected and can be a sensitive observer of what is going on. If both parents are deeply affected, perhaps a trusted friend or a professional can help.

You may want to include an older child in the planning.

Most often, parents will run the family debriefing. Plan to switch back and forth. One of you momentarily acts as participant, while the other manages the process. Pay careful attention to the kids' reactions.

If the accident was very significant for the whole family, you may want to have someone else join you to help — a sister, brother, or other close relative whom you trust.

Conduct the debriefing soon . . . within 24 to 48 hours after the accident. A debriefing is most effective if you can do it before everyone goes to sleep the first night after the accident . . . like Brad and Judith did. Sleep is the time when the mind consolidates everything that has happened during the day. Therefore, it helps to have the soothing (and correcting) discussion the debriefing offers before everyone's first sleep after the accident.

If someone is in the hospital, do it without them. Or if they are able and willing, do it there in the hospital room. But check with the doctor first.

Find a time when the family can all be together. Choose a safe and familiar place. If the kids are young, gather the family on your big double bed. If one child is resistant, let that one stay on the periphery for the moment. Very young children can participate, even if only as observers. Watching the family come together . . . living through a powerful reaction . . . surviving and prospering . . . makes each family member healthier. So make it safe and do it in sequence.

Step One
First, have everyone talk about exactly where they were when the accident happened.

I was driving.
I was in the passenger seat.
I was in the back seat behind Mom.
I was home with Grandma.

Then go around the group and have everyone tell just what they saw. Like *Dragnet*, you want the *facts* and nothing but the facts. Though many were in the same car experiencing the same accident, each person's perceptions may be very different. Start with the kids. Let them tell what they saw, but not what they felt or what it means. You want to gently immerse yourselves in this. If a child gets upset, comfort him or her and move on to the next child, coming back to the upset child later.

What should emerge from this phase of the debriefing is a complete picture that everyone in the family shares. If the children report something at odds with what you think happened, don't correct them. When your turn comes, describe the accident as you saw it. Let them hear the differences and decide for themselves what they want to make of it. If that difference in perception is important, you can deal with it later. This is a time to just listen.

Step Two

After everyone has finished with the facts, give everyone an opportunity to talk about their *first thought* during the accident. What did they think was happening or going to happen? What popped into their minds?

You are gently entering the "pool" of personal reactions one step at a time, getting adjusted and sharing it together. You started with the shallow water of the facts.

Now you are wading in further with thoughts. Let each child and adult share their first thought. No one is required to talk, but everyone is encouraged to join in. Just listening can be a big help too.

Step Three

Next, the family members discuss reactions. Now you will move from what you each thought about the accident to what you feel. Everyone is encouraged to talk about what they felt at the time — scared, terrified, anxious — whatever it was. Some kids — and even parents — will think they have no feelings about the accident. They may not be able to talk about them right then, but they do have feelings. If not much feeling is being expressed, you may want to ask, "What was the worst thing about the accident?" Here the parents' roles are both to share their own feelings and to help each of the other family members share theirs.

Now ask family members to talk about the signs of reactions they noticed in themselves, in their behavior, thoughts, feelings, and bodies. They can talk about reactions at the scene, or within the first few hours. If the debriefing is held later, talk about reactions during the first few days. Then deal with reactions now.

Step Four

After having devoted time to emotional reactions, it is time to tie them up. You can do this in several ways. Note the similarities in the reactions that family members had. You can also comment on ways in which these are common and expected reactions that everyone has. This is a good time to talk about how those feelings get better and what the kids can do about them (feeling them and sharing them with others). Stress that you will be there for your children.

Step Five

Finally, wrap things up by asking if there are questions, unresolved issues that have to be dealt with. This is a good time for a family plan. Decide together what steps you are going to take (like a visit to the friend who was in the car with you but is still in the hospital) and how you are going to care for one another. Perhaps you will make sure that you all have dinner together for the next few nights.

By talking about the accident in stages, your kids get to take some control of their experience. The accident and their reactions get validated; it all really did happen. Misconceptions are laid to rest. Kids learn that they can separate the facts from their reactions. They learn they are not alone in their reactions. The family can face not only the physical but also the emotional realities, and survive.

SUMMARY

Kids are the barometer of what is going on in a family. "Protecting" them can prolong their reactions to an accident. A special family meeting called a debriefing hastens recovery for the whole family . . . and helps you grow together.

[20] The original concept of debriefing for critical incidents and the formulation of the broad outline came from Dr. Jeffrey Mitchell and his work with emergency services workers.

19

Things You Can Do Right Now

Coping well with car accident stress is not automatic. You can benefit from what others have learned. Despite how strong some of your reactions are, you are not "crazy" or mentally ill. But you have had some strong reactions, and you are going to have others.

Here are some things you can do to smooth the recovery process.

Know What You Are Up Against

If you haven't done so, measure your car accident Stress Bill. Turn to the Stress Bill scale on page 20 and fill it out. When you discover the emotional bill that the accident has left you, you may be relieved to know how well you are doing. You will also be more aware of the resources you have at your disposal. Then you can decide if you want to take charge of your recovery or let your reactions drive you.

Crisis or Opportunity

Decide whether you are going to view the accident as a crisis or an opportunity. At first, it will feel like a crisis and won't seem to be much of an opportunity. But it is essential that you think about this decision. If you see the changes demanded by the accident as a threat, it will be a crisis. If you are willing to stretch a bit and grow, the accident can be an opportunity. The choice is yours.

If you want to look at the accident as an opportunity and

have decided you are willing to learn, think of the people you know who have faced a real crisis. Is there anyone you respect for how they handled a crisis? If so, ask that person to be your guide. Ask them what was important as they look back now.

Make the Replay Time Productive

The thoughts that keep popping into your head are a sign of your mind pressing you to figure out what happened (and what it means). Instead of resisting, learn how to help yourself along by planning times when it's OK to think through these things . . . and take a break until then. Talk with someone who has been through an accident. Pick someone to talk with who you can trust to just listen, rather than to overreact or to try to fix it for you. Set aside a specific time to talk or think about what happened and what it means. Then use that time to think it through . . . for only that specific period of time. You don't have to come up with all the answers today.

If you take control and set aside the time, you can then feel free to distract yourself. You will feel it's OK not to think or talk about the accident now because you have set aside a specific time later to deal with it.

Take a Time Out from Your Superman or Wonder Woman Side

Give yourself a break. Let yourself use the support around you. It's OK to be taken care of. Find out how to ask for what you need. Recovery is speeded up when you can find ways to take some genuine time out. That's why you should take an inventory and then put it away. (For more on taking an inventory, see the mini-guide at the end of this chapter.)

Track Your Reactions

Pay attention to your reactions. Note how they change from day to day and week to week. One good way to track them is to keep a brief journal. Just jot down what you note about your thoughts and reactions today. Don't worry if you have skipped a day. Review your journal every week or so. (If you want more information on journaling, see the Progoff entry in the recommended reading list.)

The following are stress busters that will ease your mind as you journey through your reactions. You will find other recommendations in the What to Do sections scattered throughout the book. Look up the particular reaction you are concerned with in the index and turn to that page.

---

18 Stress Busters [21]

Some other survivor has found each one of these stress busters helpful. On your journey, you will find the stress busters which work for you. Most of these suggestions will work with nightmares, flashbacks, grief, fear, anxiety, and depression. Of course, when any reaction gets out of hand, it's time to let a professional help.

1. Let your feelings out.
Call a supportive friend, someone you trust, and talk about your feelings or your problems, specifically and honestly. Sharing the load makes it lighter. Can't reach anyone? Keep calling others until you reach somebody.

2. Share your fears.
Don't be afraid to talk to people about the situations that concern you. Request help in managing those situations. Ask if a neighbor would mind picking up a few things for you at the market, because you don't feel quite up to driving or even riding there yet. If you must go out, ride with friends. Be creative.

---

3. Let go of being in control.

Fighting to forget the negative thoughts or memories that keep coming back gives them more power. Be willing to learn what they mean.

4. Learn from other people.

Read articles and books on grief and recovery. See the recommended readings. Use the index to find topics that apply to your personal situation. Get a lift from other people's experiences by listening to audiotapes and watching videotapes. See the recommended reading list.

5. Take an inventory.

See the guide at the end of the chapter. Which of the things on this list would help? Are you doing them?

6. Make a gratitude list.

Focus for a few minutes on what you have to be thankful for instead of wishing for what you lost. Write down the names of the people who *care* about you, *like* you, *love* you. Count the miracles that have happened to you, including your survival. Compare where you are now with where you were right after the accident happened. Your progress will probably startle you.

7. Make a worry list.

Include all the things that are bothering you, then cross off those that you don't have to solve today. You can worry about those tomorrow. Next to the remaining worries, note what steps you can take to deal with them. Then start dealing.

8. Try distraction.

If you have made time for reflection, get away from your

problems for a little while. Allow yourself something you enjoy — a crossword puzzle, a jigsaw puzzle, a video, a game of cards, needlepoint, a book that relaxes you, or a hobby (if you don't have one, find one). Or tackle something that needs doing — letter writing, closet cleaning, dog grooming. Weed the garden or clean the shower tiles. Make sure that what you choose will keep you busy and distracted. List what needs to be done and smile as you cross things off.

9. Try inspiration.
Listen to soothing music, drive to the water, sit in the grass and take in the sunset (or the sunrise), hike in the woods and look at the leaves. Drop in at a church, temple, or mosque you have never visited. Sit quietly for 10 minutes and listen to your inner voice.

10. Try exertion.
Go for a walk, a jog, a bike ride, a swim; shoot some hoops. Make it fun and healthy. Get your body moving. Then arrange to do it again. Or you can cross another item off your to-do list by raking leaves, chopping wood, or washing windows. Use physical activity as much as you can. It can help work off some reactions and keep you in shape for what you have to face. If you are feeling down, get up and out. Even if you are bedridden, there is some exercise you can do. Moving a finger, a toe, or an eyebrow can help. Make a prime ally of your physical therapist.

11. Try relaxation.
Try progressive relaxation, giving your system an instant vacation. (For more, see the mini-guide.) Try any activity that helps you unwind — watching birds, tending the garden, or fishing. Treat yourself to a massage, a hot

bath, a long drive, or a short nap.

12. Try meditation.
Take your mind on a vacation. Do a favorite meditation. If meditation is new, see the mini-guide for a suggestion. Another superb alternative is listening to the tape called *The Clear Plastic Bag*. (It's listed in the recommended readings.)

13. Try supplication.
Prayer, especially the Serenity Prayer (on page 159), can work wonders. Listen for the inner voice of your Higher Power, however you interpret it.

14. Try manipulation.
Of your diet, that is. Sugar can amplify bouts of depression or anxiety. Cutting down on it may lift your attitude.

15. Try invention.
Be creative. Build something, paint, sculpt, cook, compose a melody, or write a poem or short story (perhaps drawing on your experience in the accident, like Megan did at the start of the book). You can turn something bad into something useful.

16. Try a little tenderness.
Be kind to yourself; you deserve it. Share something special with your spouse, partner, family, or friend.

17. Turn it over.
Turn whatever it is you can't handle over to that Power greater than yourself. This is not a cop-out, instead it's a **way** out.

> **18. Take another measure.**
> Reflect and tell yourself how far you have come since the accident.

One Day at a Time

What you react to or want to avoid today, whatever feels overwhelming now, will not remain the same. Next week or a month from now, you will feel differently. If you don't want to ride in a car today, that's OK. You have plenty of time to ride later. If you allow yourself to make absolute statements, you box yourself in and close off options. Be flexible. Today, cross only those bridges you must.

> ### Mini-Guide — Breathing Exercises
>
> This is a wonderful exercise for times when you feel panicky or tension makes your breath catch or go shallow.
>
> Lie on your back and relax. Place one hand on your tummy and the other on your chest. If the hand on your chest is moving up and down, it means you are breathing through your chest. Try taking a deeper breath and drawing it deeper into your tummy. Keep drawing deeper breaths until you feel the hand on your tummy begin to move up and down. Each time, blow the air out of your mouth, and then let your tummy really fill with air.
>
> Watch your breathing. Let the air flow in and out. Imagine yourself taking in calmness, peace, love, and hope. Let go of all the things you don't need as you breathe out. Visualize all the fear, tension, and strain flowing out.
>
> Let your mind float and don't pay attention to any one

thought. Keep this up for eight to ten minutes.

Mini-Guide — Progressive Relaxation[22]

Start by making yourself as comfortable as you can. If possible, find a place to lie down where you will not be disturbed. Remove your shoes and loosen any tight clothing.

Clear your mind and pay no attention to stray thoughts.

Focus on your breathing. Feel the air flowing in and out.

Now focus on your feet. First, clench your toes as tightly as you can. Hold that squeeze for a few moments. Feel the tension. Now release your toes and let the tension flow out of your feet and away. Feel it go.

Arch the balls of your feet. Hold and release.
Stretch your ankles out full length, pointing your feet. Hold and release.

Now tighten the calves of your legs. Hold and release. Feel the tension flow out through your feet.

Lock your knees and tighten your thigh muscles. Hold and release.

Now tighten your buttocks. Squeeze as tightly as you can. Hold it and then release.

Tighten your stomach muscles. Hold and release. Feel the tension flow out through your feet.

Now pull your elbows into your sides, squeeze your shoulder blades together, and tighten your back muscles as tight as you can. Hold and release.

Focus on your arms and hands. First, take your fingers and, starting from the ends, curl each joint down on the next. Then roll the fingers down into your palm and make a fist. Squeeze it tight. Hold and release. Let the tension roll out of your fingers, into the floor.

Now stretch your fingers out as wide and open as you can make them.

Bend your fingers and wrists in toward your forearms as far as you can stretch them. Feel the tension. Hold and release.

Lock your elbows and tighten your arms. Hold and release.

Now make a muscle like a circus strongman with your upper arms. Tighten that muscle. Hold and release the tension.

Scrunch your shoulders up to your ears. Feel the tension. Hold and release.

Now stretch your neck, first to one side, then to the other. Lean your head forward, touching your chin to your chest. Hold and release.

Scrunch your face into a tight ball. Tense all your muscles, scrunching your eyes, nose, and mouth together. Feel the tension. Hold it and then release. Let all the tension flow out.

Now take a deep breath. Take in some more air, stretch your chest, hold that breath for a few moments, then blow it out. Repeat this.

Relax and let all the tension out. Feel your body sink into the floor. With your eyes closed and completely relaxed, let your mind float for a few moments. Don't dwell on anything. Just observe what flows through your mind. Remain floating for a few moments.

When you are ready, allow yourself to focus on where you are. With your eyes still closed, begin to focus on the air and the room around you, the rug underneath you.

When you are ready, slowly open your eyes and come back to the present, relaxed and refreshed.

You may combine the relaxation exercise with the breathing exercises or a meditation. Create a routine that suits you.

Mini-Guide — Meditation

Meditation takes practice. Try combining meditation with the relaxation exercise at first and just let your mind relax. If meditating doesn't feel smooth at first, don't worry. If you keep practicing, you will "get" it.

At first, choose a quiet place to meditate. Later you will find you can meditate even in a train car full of people.

Set aside a quiet time each day to meditate. For some people, early in the morning is best. Others favor late at night before going to sleep. Some people like to meditate while walking or even vacuuming.

If you want, try a soft musical tape — peaceful and calming. It can be soothing music or a special tape of natural sounds, waves, a breeze . . . anything that gets you in the right mood.

Before you begin, empty your mind of thoughts. You can do this by using the breathing exercises or the relaxation exercises, or just close your eyes and count back from 100.

Create a sequence that works for you. Try imagining walking down a flight of stairs and emerging into your special place.

Imagine a place you find peaceful. It can be a mountain meadow with a quiet stream nearby. Picture a beautiful sandy beach at sunset where you are all alone. Imagine yourself skipping along the wet sand. Stop, bend down, and trace a big number 10 in the sand. Visualize the wet sand curling up as your finger traces the numbers. Feel the texture of the sand against your finger as you draw. Imagine the warmth of the fading sun, a cool breeze floating by you. Then skip down a few paces, pause and carve a number 9. Notice the shifts in shading as the water filters through the sand. Feel the foamy surf curl over your toes as you skip. Then slow down and continue writing down 8 — 7 — 6 — 5. At each number notice some new detail, a shell, a sand castle left behind . . . a palm tree swaying gently. 4 — 3 — 2. Imagine that as you draw the number 1 you find a nice comfy spot and settle in on the beach. Curl up and watch the waves lap in, the puffy clouds against the deep blue sky, the sun deepening red as it sinks to the west.

Now you are ready to meditate.

Now draw on your theme. Remember a meditation thought from a favorite book you read earlier. Perhaps you heard someone make an observation that struck you. Use a line from an old song. Review the past few days. . . or meditate on what you look forward to facing today. See the obstacles and think how you can handle them differently, successfully, effortlessly. You may want to have a conversation with your Higher Power, your guardian angel, your great-grandfather.

Let your mind drift as you let that thought resonate in your head. Follow it where it leads. If this is difficult at first, listen to a meditation tape or a recorded message by someone you respect. Just let it flow.

You can also use the time to take an inventory. How have I been doing? Am I focusing my energies in the way I want? What else could I do? Where would I like to end up on this journey? Is there something I could gain?

When you have reached the end of your meditation, reverse the process. Carve the numbers upward in the sand. Climb back up the imaginary stairs. Count from 1 to 10. As you return, gradually come back to awareness of your surroundings. When you reach your destination, open your eyes and savor how refreshed you feel.

It matters less whether you meditate for 3 minutes or 30 than that you are willing to continue to practice.

A great meditation is described in *The Clear Plastic Bag*. For more information on meditation, pick up *The New Three Minute Meditator* by David Harp. Both are listed in the recommended readings.

Mini-Guide — Inventory [23]

Take an inventory. Use a couple of sheets of paper and draw a line down the middle from top to bottom.

At the top of the left-hand column, write Challenges. On the top of the right-hand column, write Resources.

Next, list each challenge you are facing. It actually helps to put them down in black and white. Put down all the pressing issues — surgery, recovery from injuries, loss of a loved one, living alone or with someone missing, repairing a car, or filing an insurance claim for the loss. List the whole "package" of reactions you notice about yourself — sleep pattern changes, fears, irritations. List them whether they seem connected with the accident or not. Next, list tasks that have to be done: phone calls, forms to fill out, hassles to deal with, the people you have to cope with. Don't try to put items in order yet or to judge them. Just list them as they come to you and add any others later that occur to you.

Now list the resources you have to deal with each challenge — your personal qualities, your strengths, the people you can count on, and the things left intact and not affected by the accident. Don't be hampered by the voice in your head that may tell you that a resource doesn't mean much or won't help now anyway. List all your resources without judging, rating, inflating, or dismissing any of them. Add others later as they occur to you.

Now look back at the challenges. Put a star next to each challenge that must be addressed today or tomorrow. Also star any signs like nightmares, tears, fears, or anxieties that feel pressing.

Now you are ready to set priorities for your challenges. Assign a number 1 next to the most pressing challenge and a number 2 to the one close behind. Continue until all the starred entries have been numbered.

Face the first challenge. Decide what you want to do about that challenge and how you plan to do it. See if the challenge is addressed in this book. Look in What's in This Book or the index. Read how other people have handled similar challenges.

If that challenge feels too overwhelming right now, that's OK. It won't be that way forever. Stretch your bag of tricks, ask for advice and help from someone you trust. Tell your ally your thoughts and ask if they agree with how you see the challenge and how you might get help. Listen to their response. Then find the answer in your heart of hearts. Is there a piece of that challenge you can face today? Good! Do that. If the challenge seems overwhelming, focus only on what has to be done and what can be done. Be gentle with yourself. Examining your resource list might help.

When you have overcome a challenge, put a red check mark at the end. If it's an ongoing challenge, add a check mark every time you do something about it.

When you've done as much as you can do today, put your list in a folder and put it away. It's all there . . . you can take it out when you need it next. For now, be grateful for what you've been able to do today and take a break.

SUMMARY

The accident was stressful. You may even feel overwhelmed by it. There are steps you can take right now to ease the stress. There are stress busters and helpful coping tips that you can put to use today.

[21] These recommendations are adapted from *The Recovery Book* (1993) by Al Mooney, M.D., Arlene Eisenberg, and Howard Eisenberg, published by Workman Publishing, New York.

[22] You may modify this exercise to suit your situation. If you are in bed in a cast, use those parts that are not in a cast. Pay attention to any limitations you have and respect them. If you have questions, ask your doctor or physical therapist. If you can't lie on the floor or a bed, use a comfortable chair. Make this your own mini-spa.

[23] If injuries restrict you, consider two alternatives. First, decide whether it's time yet to cope with everything you face or put your energy into the first part of your physical recovery. If you are ready to take a stab at the inventory, get someone you trust to write it down for you. Ask that person to refrain from any comment and to serve only as your pen.

I hope this first volume of *Car Accident: A Practical Recovery Manual* has been helpful to you . . . that it made your burden lighter or that understanding the recovery process made it easier to bear. Some recommendations may have really helped, other ideas may simply make sense. You may disagree about some opinions expressed in this book. What matters is that you have found information and strategies that help you recover.

This has been your journey. You found many gifts which illuminate your path. Your point of view has shifted. Decide now how you will share those blessings you have received.

If the accident left a high stress bill, the second volume in this set, which covers later or lingering reactions, should be equally helpful.

I welcome your comments, questions, and observations, even though I may not be able to respond to all of them.

If you have gained support in your journey and the book has helped smooth a difficult voyage, pass your wisdom on by aiding other accident survivors in their passage. Your experience, strength, and hope will guide and nourish you both.

You may write to the address on bottom of the last page or e-mail us at jackstress@spress.com.

Recommended Readings, Audiotapes, and Videotapes

Anger

Hankins, Gary, with Hankins, Carol. (1988) *Prescription for Anger: Coping with Angry Feelings and Angry People.* Warner Books. ISBN 0-446-36392-8

Children

Grollman, Earl A. (1990) *Talking About Death: A Dialogue Between Parent and Child.* Beacon Press. ISBN 0-8070-2363-9

Shafer, Dan, and Lyons, Christine. (1993) *How Do We Tell the Children?* (revised ed.). Newmarket Press, (212) 832-3575. ISBN 1-55704-181-4
Helps parents explain death to children at different age levels.

Debriefing

Grollman, Earl A. (ed.) (1967) *Explaining Death to Children.* Beacon Press. ISBN 0-8070-2385-X
What specialists recommend to ease the first confrontation with death for a child.

Mitchell, Jeffrey, and Bray, Grady. (1990) *Emergency Services Stress.* Prentice Hall. ISBN 0-89303-687-0
See Chapter 7, "Critical Incident Stress Debriefing."

Depression

Burns, David D. (1980) *Feeling Good: The New Mood Therapy.* New American Library. ISBN 0-451-13586-5

Fiction

Banks, Russell. (1991) *The Sweet Hereafter.* Harper Collins. ISBN 0-06-016703-3
The story of a town and, in particular, a school bus driver involved in an accident in which 14 children are killed.

Lott, Brett. (1993) *Reed's Beach.* Pocket Books. ISBN 0-671-79238-5
One day in the recovery of parents whose 7-year-old son was killed by a car as he was getting off the school bus.

Grief

Brooks, Anne M. (1985) *The Grieving Time: A Year's Account of Recovery from Loss.* Dial Press. ISBN 0-385-19801-9
Once-a-month journal entries for a year following her husband's death from cancer.

James, John W., and Cherry, Frank. (1988) *The Grief Recovery Handbook: A Step-by-Step Program for Moving Beyond Loss.* Perennial Library/Harper & Row. ISBN 0-06-091586-2

Kübler-Ross, Elisabeth. (1969) *On Death and Dying.* Collier. ISBN 0-02-089130-X

Lord, Janice Harris. (1991) *No Time for Goodbyes: Coping with Sorrow, Anger and Injustice After a Tragic Death.* Pathfinder Publishing. ISBN 0-934793-40-9

Journaling

Progoff, Ira. (1975) *At a Journal Workshop: The Basic Text & Guide for Using the Intensive Journal Process.* Dialogue House. ISBN 0-87941-003-5

Loss and Injury

Lord, Janice Harris. (1988) *Beyond Sympathy: What to Say and Do for Someone Suffering an Injury, Illness or Loss.* Pathfinder Publishing. ISBN 0-934793-21-2

Wheeler, Eugenie G., and Dace-Lombard, Joyce. (1988) *Living Creatively with Chronic Illness: Transcending the Loss, Pain and Frustration.* Pathfinder Publishing. ISBN 0-934793-17-4

Meditation

Harp, David. (1990) *The New Three Minute Meditator* (revised ed.). New Harbinger. ISBN 0-934986-95-9

The Clear Plastic Bag. Global Relationship Center, 16101 Stewart Road, Austin, TX 78734, (512) 266-3333. (Audiotape)

Relaxation

Benson, Herbert, with Klipper, Miriam Z. (1975) *The Relaxation Response.* Avon Books. ISBN 0-380-00676-6

Values and Spirituality

Frankl, Viktor E. (1984) *Man's Search for Meaning* (3rd ed.). Touchstone Books. ISBN 0-671-24422-1
From the most devastating circumstances come the most compelling testaments to life and meaning.

Kushner, Harold S. (1981) *When Bad Things Happen to Good People.* Avon Books. ISBN 0-380-60392-6
Provocative and comforting answers to the universal question: "Why me?"

FILMS ON VIDEOTAPE

For Younger Children

The Death of a Friend: Helping Children Cope with Grief & Loss. 15 minutes, color. Judge Baker Program, Judge Baker Children's Center, 295 Longwood Avenue, Boston, MA 02115.
Two puppets discuss their fears and worries when their friend is killed by a car. The film talks about the sadness, anger, and confusion they feel when a friend dies.

Where Is Dead? 19 minutes, color. Encyclopedia Britannica Educational Corporation, 425 North Michigan Avenue, Chicago, IL 60611.
A wonderful illustration of the dynamics of grief, mourning, and adjustment in the story of a 6-year-old girl who learns to cope with the sudden death of her older brother.

For Adults and Older Children

But He Was Only Seventeen. 35 minutes, color. Batesville Management Services, P.O. Box 90, Batesville, MD 47006.
Peer reactions to the sudden death of a 17-year-old boy who is killed in a car accident. A National Education Film Festival Finalist.

The Doctor. (1991) Directed by Randa Haines. Buena Vista/Touchstone. VHS
Fine portrayal of the process of digestion, reflection, and distraction over the news of cancer and the adjustment in a surgeon who never believed that any of this "touchy-feely mumbo-jumbo" was important.

Ordinary People. (1980) Directed by Robert Redford. Paramount Home Video. VHS 8964
Reactions reverberate through a family after a son is killed in a boating accident. Excellent portrayal of stress reactions and recovery.

For Adults

Passion Fish. (1992) Directed by John Sayles. Columbia Tri-Star Home Video. VHS 53283
Great presentation of the challenges of coming to terms with severe injury and the spiritual journey of recovery.

Sophie's Choice. (1982) Directed by Alan J. Pakula. CBS Fox Video. VHS 9076
Adaptation of the William Styron novel about a Polish Catholic woman after a concentration camp. Wonderful if sad portrayal of the workings of personal responsibility.

Bibliography

Belsky, Jay. (1989) Ordeal on I-80. About Men (column). *The New York Times Magazine*, February 19, 1989, p. 24.

Brett, Elizabeth A., and Ostroff, Robert. (1985) Imagery and Posttraumatic Stress Disorder: An Overview. *American Journal of Psychiatry* 142:4, 417-424.

Brett, Elizabeth A.; Spitzer, Robert L.; and Williams, Janet B.W. (1988) DSM-IIIR Criteria for Posttraumatic Stress Disorder. *American Journal of Psychiatry* 145:10, 1232-1236.

Brom, Daniel; Kleber, Rolf J.; and Defares, Peter B. (1985) Brief Psychotherapy for Posttraumatic Stress Disorders. *Journal of Consulting & Clinical Psychology* 57:5, 607-612.

Burstein, Allan. (1985) How Common Is Delayed Posttraumatic Stress Disorder? *American Journal of Psychiatry* 142:7, 887.

Burstein, Allan. (1986) Can Monetary Compensation Influence the Course of a Disorder? *American Journal of Psychiatry* 143:1, 112.

Burstein, Allan; Ciccone, Patrick E.; Greenstein, Robert A.; Daniels, E., et al. (1988) Chronic Vietnam PTSD and Acute Civilian PTSD: A Comparison of Treatment Experiences. *General Hospital Psychiatry* 10:4, 245-249.

Connelly, Peter J., and Gilmour, Fergus. (1989) Munchausen Syndrome: New Cause for Concern. *Journal of Clinical Psychiatry* 50:2, 73.

Culpan, R., and Taylor, C. (1973) Pyschiatric Disorders Following Road Traffic and Industrial Injuries. *Australian-New Zealand Journal of Psychiatry* 7: 32-39.

Eth, Spencer, and Pynoos, Robert S. (eds.). (1985) *Post-traumatic Stress Disorder in Children*. Washington: American Psychiatric Press.

Goldberg, Lawrence, and Gara, Michael. (1990) A Typology of Psychiatric Reactions to Motor Vehicle Accidents. *Psychopathology* 23:15-20.

Horowitz, Mardi J. (1976) *Stress Response Syndromes*. New York, Aronson.

Horowitz, Mardi J.; Becker, S.S.; and Malone, P. (1972) Intrusive Thinking in Psychiatric Patients After Stress. *Psychological Reports* 31:235-238.

Horowitz, Mardi J.; Wilner, Nancy; and Alvarez, W. (1979) Impact of Event Scale: A Measure of Subjective Stress. *Psychosomatic Medicine* 41:209-218.

Hudson, Charles J., and Pilek, Eugene. (1990) PTSD in the Retarded. *Hospital and Community Psychiatry* 41:1, 97.

Interministerial Task Force on Motor Vehicle Accident Injuries. (1981). Injury: An Ontario Survey of the Societal and Personal Costs of Hospitalized Motor Vehicle Accident Victims. Ontario Ministry of Transportation and Communications.

Jones, I. H., and Riley, W. T. (1987) The Post Accident Syndrome: Variations in the Clinical Picture. *Australian-New Zealand Journal of Psychiatry* 21:560-567.

Kuch, Klaus; Swinson, Richard P.; and Kirby, Marlene. (1985) Post-Traumatic Stress Disorder After Car Accidents. *Canadian Journal of Psychiatry* 30:10, 426-427.

Lazarus, Richard S. (1966) *Psychological Stress and the Coping Process*. New York, McGraw Hill.

Lazarus, Richard S. (1977) Cognitive and Coping Processes in Emotion. In Alan Monat and Richard S. Lazarus (eds.). *Stress and Coping: An Anthology*. New York, Columbia University Press.

Lees-Haley, Paul R. (1986) Pseudo Post Traumatic Stress Disorder. *Trial Diplomacy Journal* 9:4, 17-20.

Milgram, Norman A.; Toubiana, Yosef H.; Klingman, Avigdor; Raviv, Amiram, et al. (1988) Situational Exposure and Personal Loss in Children's Acute and Chronic Stress Reactions. *Journal of Traumatic Stress* 1:3, 339-352.

Modlin, Herbert C. (1960) The Trauma in "Traumatic Neurosis." *Bulletin of the Menninger Clinic* 24:2, 49-56.

Parker, Neville. (1977) Accident Litigants with Neurotic Symptoms. *Medical Journal of Australia* 1977:2, 318-321.

Platt, Jerome J., and Husband, Stephen D. (1986) Post-traumatic Stress Disorder in Forensic Practice. *American Journal of Forensic Psychology* 4:1, 29-56.

Platt, Jerome J., and Husband, Stephen D. (1987) Post-traumatic Stress Disorder and the Motor Vehicle Accident. *American Journal of Forensic Psychology* 5:2, 35-42.

Sloan, Patrick. (1988) Post-traumatic Stress in Survivors of an Airplane Crash Landing: A Clinical and Experimental Research Intervention. *Journal of Traumatic Stress* 1:2, 211-229.

Smith, Elizabeth M.; North, Carol S.; McCool, Robert E.; and Shea, James M. (1990) Acute Postdisaster Psychiatric Disorders: Identification of Persons at Risk. *American Journal of Psychiatry* 147:2, 202-206.

Walker, John I. (1981) Posttraumatic Stress Disorder After a Car Accident. *Postgraduate Medicine* 69:2, 82-86.

Zilberg, N.J.; Weiss, Daniel S.; and Horowitz, Mardi J. (1982) Impact of Event Scale: A Cross-validational Study and Some Empirical Evidence Supporting a Conceptual Model of Stress Response Syndromes. *Journal of Consulting & Clinical Psychology* 50:407-414.

Many Thanks

A book like this is not the product of one person. A whole team has contributed to this book. With love and admiration, my deepest thanks go to:

Adele, Al, Alexander, Amy, Angelia, Ann, Anna, Art, Barbara, Benson, Beth, Betty, Bill, Bob, Bonnie, Bruce, Callie, Carolyn, Chad, Charles, Chris, Chuck, Clurie, Connie, Danny, Dave, Dawn, David, Dee, Dick, Don, Donna, Ed, Eddie, Eileen, Erline, Ernestine, Flo, Gene, Graham, Gretchen, Harriet, Ilana, J.D., Jack, James, Janice, Jean, Jeffrey, Jen, Jessica, Jim, Joe, John, Jonathan, Jose, Kathy, Kate, Kay, Kip, Laurie, Lea, Ligi, Linda, Louis, Margit, Marge, Margo, Marilyn, Mary, Megan, Melissa, Michael, Mike, Mollye, Nancy, Natasha, Norma, Patrice, Pat, Paul, Pete, Peter, Reggie, Rena, Richard, Rick, Roger, Roseann, Sam, Sally, Sarah, Shelley, Susan, Terri, Tig, Tom, Tony, Vickie, Walter, and Warner for sharing your pain, your courage, and your determination as well as your stories, and for enriching my life.

To George Moore, Bob Lifton, Hy Shatan, Herman Engel, Florence Volkman-Pincus, Steve Kadish, Les Wyman, and Brenda and Evan Turner, who helped me see the gifts and were willing to nurture the faintest of lights.

To the Angels — Al and Betty Smith, Sam and Maria Miller, Chuck and Sandy Abookire, Erline Belton, Graham Grund, Toby Devan Lewis, Kevin and Ellen O'Donnell, Ed and Sarah Roth, and Bert and Therese Smith, who made it possible.

To the Fans—Jack and Mebbie Brown, Don Doskey, Bonnie Humphrey, Neal and Nancy Lavelle, Bill and Ruth Sawyer, Janet Sawyer, Steve and Trudi Weisenberger, and Larry Wheeler, who helped it along.

To Chad Worcester, Brenda Turner, Candace McKinley, Adele Silver, and Judith Stein, who took the book apart and lovingly put it together.

To Ann Sethness, my loving partner, who agreed to come fly with me, kept faith in the wilderness, and nurtured every aspect of this project with devotion to a higher good.

To all those who ever asked, "How is the book coming?"

Copyright Acknowledgments

Index

Ordering Additional Copies of

Car Accident:
A Practical Recovery Manual
*for Drivers, Passengers, and
the People in Their Lives*

If your bookstore is unable to obtain this book,
or you need express service, you may order directly:

Consumer Orders
1-800-507-2665

Book Trade Orders
1-800-345-0096 (Phone)
1-800-950-9793 (Fax)

Mail Orders to:
Publishers Distribution Service
6893 Sullivan Road
Grawn, Michigan 49637

For Bulk Purchases contact:
StressPress Inc.
25931 Euclid Avenue #270
Cleveland, Ohio 44132
1-800-351-2612
1-216-541-3400 (Fax)